Four Days in Spring

Four Days in Spring

Christ Suffering, Dying,
and Rising in Our Lives

Herbert O'Driscoll

Judi,

Blessings.

Herb O'Driscoll

2009.

Path Books
A LIGHT TO MY PATH

ABC Publishing, Anglican Book Centre
General Synod of the Anglican Church of Canada
80 Hayden Street, Toronto, Ontario, Canada M4Y 3G2
abcpublishing@national.anglican.ca
www.abcpublishing.com www.pathbooks.com

Text set in ITC Legacy Serif and Footlight MT Light
Cover and text design by Jane Thornton
Cover image: Albrecht Altdorfer, "Resurrection of Christ," 1518

Library and Archives Canada Cataloguing in Publication
O'Driscoll, Herbert, 1928-
    Four days in spring : Christ suffering, dying, and rising in our lives / Herbert O'Driscoll.

ISBN 1-55126-493-5

    1. Lenten sermons. 2. Holy-Week sermons. 3. Holy Week--Meditations. 4. Lent--Meditations. 5. Jesus Christ--Passion. I. Title.

BV90.O37 2007   251'.62   C2006-906263-3

Printed in Canada

for Terry and Percy,
my brothers and
my good companions

Contents

Preface

The idea for this book was conceived after I read a passage from one of the addresses in Archbishop Rowan Williams's magnificent book, *A Ray of Darkness*. In his address entitled "Keeping Time," given at the Three Choirs Festival, the Archbishop writes,

> Each year, the church renews its understanding of itself and its world in the process, the story, of the Christian Year. Above all, in Holy Week and Easter, it takes us inexorably through a series of changing relationships, shifting perspectives, that cannot be rushed: it leads us through the Passion and Resurrection of Jesus, which is the centre and wellspring of what we are. We can't do this with selected highlights, saving time; this is a contemplation, a feeding, that requires our flesh and blood, our patience, our passion. It requires that things are done to us, that we allow ourselves to be changed and enlarged.

Reading this and being captured by it, I resolved to do something for others and for myself. I would examine the scripture passages that apply to the specific hours during which our Lord shared a meal with his disciples, was taken by his enemies, endured the horror of crucifixion, died, and moved beyond death to be present with his disciples. Those hours began sometime on the day we call Thursday, when he asked two of his friends to go into Jerusalem and confirm the booking of a room already arranged. I have traced these hours to the evening of the day we call Sunday. Thus the title, *Four Days in Spring*.

Having read and reflected on each incident during the four days, I have attempted to do two things: first, to tell the event as vividly as I could, while trying to remain true to the scripture; second, to reflect on some aspect of the endless depths of meaning hidden in the scripture. In doing this, I have had in mind a general readership, for whom this book might serve as a series of short devotional readings. I have also considered those clergy and lay readers who are responsible for preaching homilies, as well as those who lead Bible study groups.

Far from being an ending, those four days in spring were a beginning. What began would grow and spread through the world and through time, until it would come to you and me as the gift of Christianity and the community of faith we call the church.

In his own time Paul of Tarsus was aware of the great gift he had been given. He expressed his gratitude by noting all the encounters with the risen Christ of which he was aware, then completing that list of encounters by saying, "Last of all, as to one untimely born, he appeared also to me." Writing these pages has been a spiritual experience. If becoming deeply aware of the cost paid for my faith is to experience an encounter with the risen Lord, then I would claim such an experience. If my reflections make such an encounter possible for those who read them, then I shall be grateful.

No book is written without there being a sense of gratitude to others. To my wife, Paula, who understands what it means to live with a spouse present in body but absent in spirit for long periods—not too absent, however, to appreciate cups of coffee and tea and sundry accompanying good things! As always, my thanks to Robert Maclennan for his ever gentle but firm editing and generous guidance.

"I pray," wrote Paul to the community in Ephesus, "that you may have the power to comprehend, with all the saints, what is the breadth and length and height, and depth, and to know the love of Christ that passes knowledge."

Victoria, B.C.
August 2006

❦ ONE ❦

Prologue

Let the same mind be in you that was in Christ Jesus, who, though he was in the form of God, did not regard equality with God as something to be exploited, but emptied himself, taking the form of a slave, being born in human likeness. And being found in human form, he humbled himself and became obedient to the point of death—even death on a cross. Therefore God also highly exalted him and gave him the name that is above every name, so that at the name of Jesus every knee should bend, in heaven and on earth and under the earth, and every tongue should confess that Jesus Christ is Lord, to the glory of God the Father. (Philippians 2:5–11)

This morning I am scheduled to be with a group of clergy who will be visiting the Church of Saint Peter in Gallicantu, Jerusalem. They have already left the college with another staff member and will be seeing other places in the city before they arrive at Saint Peter's.

Estimating the time we are likely to meet, I take a *sherut*—an Arab taxi—and ask to be driven to the church. Saint Peter's in Gallicantu is south of the old city. Evidence suggests that on this site once stood the house of Caiaphas, the high priest who dealt with a certain prisoner from Nazareth.

When I entered the church, their instructor was still addressing the group; so I decided to wait outside. I left the church, turned right, and walked a few yards to where I could look down a long stony slope that drew my eyes first to the end of Tyropean Valley, then up the lower slopes of the Mount of Olives, and finally to its summit. What then came to mind may have derived from my familiarity with some widely held opinions about this area.

First, as I looked closely at the long slope falling away from me and the side of the church, I knew that the worn steps, now half-hidden in the thin soil and dust, had provided a way for people to climb from the lower city in our Lord's day. I could imagine him a figure on those steps, perhaps with a companion or a group. Second, as my eyes focused on the south end of the Tyropean Valley, I recalled how many people think it likely that the house where our Lord shared supper with his friends was somewhere in that area. Third, as I gazed at the slope of the Mount of Olives, today heavily built on, I imagined that two thousand years ago it would have been thickly wooded.

It was at this point that I had an experience I have never forgotten. Vivid and moving, it gave me a sense of the near presence of our Lord as few other episodes in my life have done. That Holy Thursday, which I was living out, became for me the Holy Thursday that he had had to live, a day that for him would have been full of anxiety, tension, and even dread. I began to imagine the sequence of that evening, relying on images of scripture that I had known since childhood.

I recalled how that meal in the upper room must have been made infinitely painful for him, both by the looming shadow of mortal danger and by the knowledge of his having been betrayed. Then I recalled how, at some stage late in the evening, he suggested that they leave the house and move toward the lower slopes of the garden, a public area in those days.

My thoughts at this stage became even more vivid, almost as if the chasm of time between my day and that long-ago night had closed. Scripture closely follows the events of the next few hours. At some stage Jesus seems to have changed his mind about allowing the full band of disciples to accompany him. While we have no record of the words, in some sensitive way he may have expressed a preference that only a few continue with him. Then he climbed farther up the lower mountain slope with the three he had selected—Peter, James, and John. But we see him pause yet again, turn to them, and ask that he be allowed to go on alone.

Whether he continued into the wood only a short distance—Mark speaks of him as going "a little farther"—or whether they kept him in sight in consideration of his obvious distress, we have a record of the struggle that took place in that dark rock-strewn clearing, and we know its sublime climax in the words "Not my will but yours be done."

As I stood at the railing beside that church in Gallicantu, which means "cock crow" (referring to an event that was to devastate Peter), I suddenly realized a pattern in my recollections from scripture. I became almost certain that the sequence in our Lord's behaviour—needing the company of friends, then wishing for only a few, then wanting to be alone—portrayed him struggling with a decision that he dared not share with any of them, even those nearest to him.

I looked again at the Mount of Olives, trying to imagine how it might have been that night. The lower slopes would have had pathways for public use, but the upper slopes would lead deeper and deeper into trees and undergrowth. An active thirty-year-old could reach the summit fairly quickly, had he chosen to do so. On attaining that summit, he would be free! From there he could in a couple of hours be far out in the Judean desert. It is highly unlikely that he would be pursued. A wise political authority like Caiaphas would realize that, by fleeing, Jesus had forfeited any possibility of leading a significant political or religious movement.

I cannot help but think that there must have been the temptation. If I am to accept his utter humanity, then he must have known great dread about what was approaching to destroy him. But on this day I also know that I stand here, this church stands here, and this otherwise ordinary Thursday is a Holy Thursday, because he did not give in to the temptation to flee.

After a while someone emerged from the church and signalled that I could now spend time with the group. I went in to be with them, but my experience was too close to share. Time would pass before I could speak of it.

Jerusalem: Holy Thursday, 1993

❦ TWO ❦

The Gathering

Then came the day of Unleavened Bread, on which the Passover lamb had to be sacrificed. So Jesus sent Peter and John, saying, "Go and prepare the Passover meal for us that we may eat it." They asked him, "Where do you want us to make preparations for it?" "Listen," he said to them, "when you have entered the city, a man carrying a jar of water will meet you; follow him into the house he enters and say to the owner of the house, 'The teacher asks you, "Where is the guest room, where I may eat the Passover with my disciples?"' He will show you a large room upstairs, already furnished. Make preparations for us there." So they went and found everything as he had told them; and they prepared the Passover meal. (Luke 22:7–13)

Sometime early in the day they came to him and asked if he wished them to make arrangements for the supper. He accepted the offer, but gave very careful and precise instructions as to how and where they should choose the venue. It is obvious that he had already arranged for someone to meet them, identify himself to them, and guide them to the place.

By now Jesus knew that his movements were being watched by powerful forces. We can safely assume that he was exhausted and dispirited by the events of the previous few days. He had undergone a series of daily confrontations in the public area of the temple. These confrontations had increased in intensity and ugliness. At a gathering in a Bethany home, a place where he would have felt reasonably sheltered and supported, a woman had suddenly approached him and poured a vial of expensive oil over him. The symbolism was unmistakable, and Jesus knew it. The woman was anticipating his death. Compounding this chilling presentiment was his probable knowledge that the authorities were planning to take him.

All of this would have weighed heavily on him as he greeted the disciples at the prearranged place and sat down with them at table. Something more ominous and more devastating than anything he had experienced so far was now facing him. In some way he had learned that one of the beloved circle had betrayed him to the authorities, and in doing so had betrayed all of them. It was impossible to estimate how much time was left. We can assume that Jesus was carefully choosing how he would use whatever time remained. He must now have been asking himself what he needed to reiterate and emphasize from all that he had tried to share with them in the preceding few months. Throughout these months he had become increasingly aware of the limitations of their understanding.

He would not have been human if he did not know cold

fear. Also, he would have felt a crushing disappointment at being betrayed. As he looked around the table, he may even have wondered if this group of uncomprehending and deeply dependant friends were capable of realizing his dream of a future community, living in faithfulness to the vision he had so often referred to as the kingdom of God.

As we ourselves join with others in the worship on this Maundy Thursday, we are in essence taking our place at this table. The table we see in front of us in the church may look different. It may be richly carved and elaborately dressed. Later in this liturgy its rich adornment will be removed. To some extent we will be reminded of the greater simplicity of that long-ago table. On this night all places of Christian worship, whether small parish churches or great cathedrals, reach for this simplicity.

We may be reminded also of the gift we are being given by our admission to this upper room. This is no mere nostalgic meal. We might consider the many times in our lives when the eucharist has been precious beyond price to us. We may have shared it with others in joy at a marriage or in sorrow from a great loss. We may have felt the deep bonds of family as we went forward with our children to share the bread and wine. None of these moments, with their beauty and their grace-giving power, would be available to us had Jesus not joined his friends and sat with them on this night.

We need to place ourselves among this small gathering around the table, allowing ourselves to come within his gaze as he looks around the circle of faces. We may come with many gifts and abilities, personal and professional. But here in this circle at this table, facing our Lord in the intimacy of this room, we know how limited is the faithfulness we have to offer him. Yet even as we acknowledge what an unworthy guest we are, we look across the table and meet the gaze of eyes that hold nothing but joyous welcome for us.

In spite of that loving affirmation of our presence, we need to be aware of the burden carried by this person who sits across from us. The harsh confrontations of the last few days, the sense of present enemies, perhaps the awareness of possible defeat—all these things form part of our own experience at different times.

Christian tradition speaks so much of the sufferings of Jesus that we can easily, and mistakenly, restrict our thoughts to his physical pain. Terrible though this was, we need to remember that Jesus opened himself to the entire range of stresses and traumas that we know in our own lives. The pain we sometimes bear ourselves. The pain of others whom we love yet cannot relieve. The disappointment when our most fervently held dreams and hopes remain unfulfilled. To realize this is to find a deep bond forming between his life and ours.

THREE

The Knowledge of Betrayal

*When the hour came, [Jesus] took his place at the table,
and the apostles with him.... "But see, the one who betrays
me is with me, and his hand is on the table. For the Son of
Man is going as it has been determined, but woe to that
one by whom he is betrayed!" Then they began to ask one
another, which one of them it could be who would do this.*
(Luke 22:14, 21–23)

As Jesus took his place at the table that evening, it would seem from the gospel record that one thing was uppermost in his mind. For a while he managed to contain his thoughts. His friends had begun their meal. We can assume that they shared the kind of small talk normal in any circle of friends. But under the circumstances the talk may have been inhibited and even forced. Jesus was withdrawn and uncommunicative, a sure indication that something was wrong,

When Jesus did speak, the effect was devastating. There was no gradual approach, no softening of the grim reality. Into what may have been a moment of silence in the quiet conversation, Jesus announced, "One of you will betray me."

It was like a bomb exploding in a room already full of tension. Food was forgotten. Nobody spoke. Instantly the circle was shattered by distrust. Even mutual glances must have been disturbing. Then the silence was broken. It would have been consistent with his customary role in the circle that Peter should first ask the whispered disbelieving question, "Surely, not I?"

We need to remember that Jesus had not yet defined the kind of betrayal he is speaking about. All sorts of minor guilts about unfaithfulness may have surfaced in the disciples' minds. Each would have desperately searched back over recent weeks or even months: "What did I say? What have I done? How have I failed?"

Slowly the real horror sinks in. This is no petty betrayal, no minor falling away from expected standards of behaviour. Jesus is not disappointed about some misdemeanour. The agonized questioning ceases. When they have fallen silent, Jesus speaks. It must have been obvious that every syllable was being wrung unwillingly from him. This is clearly a major betrayal. "[He] who has dipped his hand into the bowl with me will betray me."

The laws of Eastern hospitality have been transgressed. Disloyalty toward a person with whom one is sharing hospitality is the ultimate betrayal. Jesus' statement allows no illusions to remain. The silence is again broken by a quiet voice that is the last to ask, "Surely, not I, Lord?" Jesus takes a piece of bread, dips it in the oil of the dish, hands it to Judas, and for a moment speaks so quietly to him that only John, seated next to our Lord, hears and recalls the words years later. Then Judas stands, turns from the table, and leaves. John would remember that, when the door opened, "it was night."

To say that we have been betrayed is to speak intensely and powerfully. The word is rarely used in a casual way. We might admit to being deceived by someone, or being mistaken in our judgment of someone. But neither of these carries the force of being betrayed.

All human relationships depend to some degree on trust. In professional relationships with employees or colleagues, we begin by according a limited measure of trust. Only a certain amount of responsibility or finance is involved. Supervision may be applied. If the trust is broken, then the consequences are contained. As the relationship progresses, whether it be personal as in a marriage, or professional as in a business partnership, the trust grows until breaking it becomes unthinkable. If such a level of trust is indeed broken, the consequences can be dreadful. At this point we speak of being betrayed.

In recent years we have watched sadly as trust in many kinds of relationships has been broken. Some people in professional positions of authority—teachers, clergy, doctors, accountants, social workers, chief executive officers—have deeply betrayed the trust given them. So insidious has this phenomenon become that the very idea of trust has been deeply damaged, impairing the ability of institutions to function.

To some extent and in varying ways, each of us receives the trust of others. This trust is often accompanied by affection, sometimes even by love. The greatest gift we can give to another is to be found worthy of their trust. The greatest pain we can inflict is to betray their trust. Whenever we are found worthy of trust, we are fulfilling our Christian vocation, that of reflecting in our lives something of the trustworthiness of our Lord himself.

❦ FOUR ❦

The Act of a Servant

Jesus, knowing that the Father had given all things into his hands, and that he had come from God and was going to God, got up from the table, took off his outer robe, and tied a towel around himself. Then he poured water into a basin and began to wash the disciples' feet and to wipe them with the towel that was tied around him. He came to Simon Peter, who said to him, "Lord, are you going to wash my feet?" Jesus answered, "You do not know now what I am doing, but later you will understand." Peter said to him, "You will never wash my feet." Jesus answered, "Unless I wash you, you have no share with me." Simon Peter said to him, "Lord, not my feet only but also my hands and my head!" Jesus said to him, "One who has bathed does not need to wash, except for the feet, but is entirely clean. And you are clean, though not all of you." For he knew who was to betray him; for this reason he said, "Not all of you are clean." (John 13:3–11)

The issue of Jesus' disciples seeking precedence is mentioned in all four gospels. The incidents themselves differ, but the issue remains the same. Who is the greatest? Who deserves special treatment?

Both Matthew and Mark recount an incident where the two disciples James and John have obviously failed to hear anything Jesus has said about the kind of life and community to which he calls them. In different ways and at different times he has done his best to help them see that that future will exact a terrible price and will require sacrifice. Seemingly oblivious to everything Jesus has told them, the two request preferential treatment in the good times that assuredly lie ahead in their self-centred imaginations.

In his telling, Luke recalls a dispute among the disciples about who will stand above the rest, who will be greatest. The timing that Luke suggests is breathtaking in its crassness. The subject spills on to the table of their last supper together. In John's telling, an incident occurs before the bread is broken and the wine cup is lifted and passed. Jesus' response, at least initially, is not so much word as vivid action. As we read in the preceding quote from his gospel, John's remembering is extraordinarily detailed.

Jesus doesn't even ask someone to fetch the water from the doorway. He gets it himself. As he begins to wash their feet one by one, there is shocked silence. By the time he reaches Simon Peter and asks him to extend a foot, Peter is ready to explode with a mixture of embarrassment and indignation. His outburst meets a calm but adamant response. The amazing process continues until completed.

Only then does Jesus speak, spelling out clearly the reason for his act. He has come among them as servant. They must go among others as servants. If they cannot understand this, then they have understood nothing of what he has said about his vision of the kingdom of God. At one stage, he seems to acknowledge the great chasm that lies between realization and reality, between belief and action. "If you know these things," he says, "you are blessed if you do them."

We do of course know these things. We know them very well. The difficulty, as Jesus understands and points out, is putting them into practice. We live in a society where authority is always based on some aspect of power—financial, political, professional, sometimes even sexual. Where such a basis exists for authority, it frequently results in the abuse of power.

For what Jesus did—bringing to the table the water to wash away the filth of the roadway and the city street—was in itself startling. This was the very antithesis of the understanding of status, leadership, and authority that any reasonable person in that or any other society can comprehend. We have only to imagine the equivalent in a contemporary institution or corporation—a person in authority acting in a way that seems on the surface self-demeaning and embarrassing.

And yet, very often in corporate life, when someone in authority does indeed act with an unaccustomed and utterly unexpected kindness and sensitivity, people recognize that such authority is based on something deeper and more admirable than power. In such a moment, we are given a glimpse of Jesus' wisdom and vision being realized among us.

What our Lord is saying by his long-ago washing of the feet, what he spells out meticulously to that circle of half-comprehending men around the table, is this—while authority may be based on power in the world, there is another basis for authority that is far more profound. This basis is servanthood.

At a certain moment in this episode, as John the Evangelist recalls it, Jesus says something that speaks to our own Christian experience, and perhaps to the heart of all Christian experience. When he had put aside the filthy water, most probably taking it to the door of the room, as any household servant would do, he put on his outer robe. Returning to the table, he looked at them and posed one of those questions that sounds utterly simple, but in reality is timeless and penetrating. Jesus asks of them, as he asks of each one of us, "Do you know what I have done to you?"

Suddenly I realize that I do. By his death on the cross—mere hours away from this moment, kneeling before those men whom he called friends—he has washed me and made me acceptable to God in a way far beyond my deserving or understanding. He has also empowered me, freeing me from a sense of unworthiness that can often immobilize my ability to serve him. He has made it possible for me to offer myself to him.

❦ Five ❦

The Burden of Anxiety

After [Jesus] had washed their feet, had put on his robe, and had returned to the table, he said to them, "Do you know what I have done to you? You call me Teacher and Lord—and you are right, for that is what I am. So if I, your Lord and Teacher, have washed your feet, you also ought to wash one another's feet. For I have set you an example, that you also should do as I have done to you. Very truly, I tell you, servants are not greater than their master, nor are messengers greater than the one who sent them." (John 13:12–16)

When something very important is on our minds, something we feel is key to whatever future we are planning, our human nature wants to deal with lesser things first, to get them out of the way so that we can concentrate on what we regard as essential. This may be the reason our Lord did not move immediately to the great central acts of bread and wine that were to become the strong anchor of Christian life until the end of time.

As we have seen, Jesus deals first with some things that were causing him anxiety. He seems to be agonizing over the realization that his beloved circle of friends includes a traitor. Is it going too far to suggest that this development represented a learning experience for Jesus, about the potential for evil in human nature? We can assume that the betrayal of a friend would have been utterly inconceivable in his own make up. Why then should he not be devastated by encountering betrayal in another?

It is interesting to read John's recollection of the few minutes during which Jesus washed the feet of his friends. It is as if his mind could not help returning again and again to the thought that one of them was now his enemy, as if he simply could not believe it to be true. Jesus has just washed Peter's feet when he says to him, "You are clean." Then, almost as if the thought must be spoken, he adds, "though not all of you." Even from the distance of many years later, John dwells on this moment.

Later, when the washing is completed and Jesus is once again sitting at table, speaking of his reasons for his action, he makes clear that there is an unnamed exception to those whom he considers his chosen friends. His voice must have been laden with regret as he says, "I am not speaking of all of you; I know whom I have chosen." Then comes again a hint that he was finding it almost impossible to grasp this new reality. "The one who ate my bread," he says disbelievingly, "has lifted his heel against me."

A second issue, although not causing him the agony of Judas's betrayal, certainly created great anxiety for our Lord. The seeming inability of the disciples to grasp the notion of servanthood distressed him. For Jesus, this understanding was central to any future community of faith he may have envisioned. He had spoken of it on other occasions. His decision on this night not only to speak of it, but to communicate it, by carrying out the most vivid of actions, is a measure of his anxiety.

A third anxiety would surface before this evening was over. The friends would hear Jesus, as he prayed to the Father, almost pleading with them to stay united after his presence had been taken from them.

Perhaps because I know the part that anxiety plays in my own life, I am particularly aware when scripture suggests that anxiety was a real and significant element in Jesus' human experience. His admonishment not to be anxious is itself an admission that he knows the daily reality of anxiety in human life! Here on this night, when great shadows of danger, and even death, loom over everything he has tried to be and do in the years since he began his public ministry, is it any wonder that pressing anxieties would surface?

Here too is a familiar pattern in our own human nature— whenever some crisis has to be engaged, we become aware of issues that normally would be kept in the background. It is almost as if our defenses have been pierced by the crisis we face and a myriad lesser fears crowd upward into our conscious mind.

All of this would be no more than personal reflection about my own psychological make up were it not for the fact that Christian faith can make a great difference here. To know, as we deal with our anxieties, that our Lord himself shares this struggle, is to have ultimate companionship in the experience. I do not have to be ashamed of my anxiety, nor do I have in some way to feel it as an admission of little faith. All I have to do is share it with our Lord, asking not that my anxiety will be made to disappear by some magic means, but that I may have the grace of his companionship to carry it.

❦ SIX ❦

Strength in Weakness

*When [Judas] had gone out, Jesus said, "Now the Son of
Man has been glorified, and God has been glorified in him.
If God has been glorified in him, God will also glorify him
in himself and will glorify him at once. Little children, I am
with you only a little longer. You will look for me; and as I
said to the Jews so now I say to you, 'Where I am going, you
cannot come.' I give you a new commandment, that you love
one another. Just as I have loved you, you also should love
one another. By this everyone will know that you are my disciples, if you have love for one another." Simon Peter said to
him, "Lord, where are you going?" Jesus answered, "Where
I am going, you cannot follow me now; but you will follow
afterward." Peter said to him, "Lord, why can I not follow
you now? I will lay down my life for you." Jesus answered,
"Will you lay down your life for me? Very truly, I tell you,
before the cock crows, you will have denied me three times."*
(John 13:31–38)

Immediately following the departure of Judas, the pace of Jesus' efforts to communicate with the disciples quickens. From this moment there is no knowing when the final attack will come and sever his link with them.

Since the disciples had probably not heard clearly, if at all, the exchange between Jesus and Judas, our Lord's statement that "the Son of Man has been glorified" would have been incomprehensible to them. Only when he continues do they realize that he will not be with them much longer. His next statement must have come like a hammer blow: "Where I am going, you cannot come."

The reaction to this news would have been immediate and intense. At least two years had gone by, perhaps three, since the group had formed. The relationship had transformed their lives in ways that were no less real although they could not explain them. Jesus had become the centre of their lives. Even at the most difficult moments, when he had asked them if they would leave him, they had answered, "To whom shall we go?" To be told now that everything was about to end must have been devastating.

Jesus has just told them that they cannot come where he is going. Now he issues a call so demanding and ultimate that all but the highest Christian commitment falls short of it. "Love one another," he says, leaving no doubt that this, above all, should be the mark of their life together. But when Peter summons the presence of mind to respond, he entirely ignores this magnificent vision of a community characterized by mutual love. What most concerns Peter, and probably the others as well, is much more immediate. He asks simply, "Lord, where are you going?"

With infinite patience Jesus refuses to explain. Again he states clearly that Peter cannot follow. Peter's cry, which conveys all the desolation of a lost child, rings across the room.

Why can he not follow? He will do anything for Jesus, even give his life if necessary.

The echoes of Peter's cry die away. Into the silence Jesus speaks the gentlest of tones, asking his friend a devastating question: "Will you lay down your life for me?" The reality will be tragically different. Before dawn breaks there will be repeated denials. Not another sound is heard from the stricken disciple.

The more we probe the humanity of men and women in scripture, seeking out the nuances of character and motivation in their lives, the more they become real, and the more they reflect back to us the patterns of our responses to God. As we walk with them in scripture, we also see, sometimes in spite of ourselves, the ways God uses their humanity.

What can we make of this short but intense exchange across the table that night? In Peter's inability to hear Jesus' new commandment, we see our own frequent human response to life. We may have an informed and mature Christian faith, but it can suddenly pale into insignificance—at least momentarily—if we find ourselves facing a significant personal threat or crisis.

For the moment nothing else matters other than this fearful possibility—a threat to health, the ending of a relationship, a professional failure. All the defenses we erect between ourselves and our fears are pierced. We realize how vulnerable we are. We confront the huge chasm between what we aspire to be spiritually and what we really are.

As we see Peter coming painfully to the kind of self-knowledge that can be maturing and transforming, we are shown that the road to maturity passes through the difficult country of self-recognition. Many who have become valuable instruments for God's work in the world have begun by experiencing God showing them their weakness and poverty.

Jesus' warning to Peter is a warning to each one of us. At some stage in life we will discover the fragility of our faith. When we do so, we need to hear Jesus assuring Peter that he will pray for him. In that moment Peter realizes what we all need to realize—no denial, no weakness can sever the bond between our Lord and us. "Who will separate us from the love of Christ?" asks Paul, writing to the community in Rome. "No … I am convinced that [nothing] in all creation will be able to separate us from the love of God in Christ Jesus our Lord."

There is an old gospel hymn that sings of what it calls "blessed assurance." Here we have a wonderful assertion that our personal weaknesses do not—and never can—invalidate us as potential instruments of God's work in the world.

❦ SEVEN ❦

A Mature Friendship

[Jesus said,] "If I go and prepare a place for you, I will come again and will take you to myself, so that where I am, there you may be also. And you know the way to the place where I am going." Thomas said to him, "Lord, we do not know where you are going. How can we know the way?" Jesus said to him, "I am the way, and the truth, and the life. No one comes to the Father except through me. If you know me, you will know my Father also. From now on you do know him and have seen him." Philip said to him, "Lord, show us the Father, and we will be satisfied." Jesus said to him, "Have I been with you all this time, Philip, and you still do not know me? Whoever has seen me has seen the Father. How can you say, 'Show us the Father'? Do you not believe that I am in the Father and the Father is in me?" (John 14:3–10a)

Jesus could not fail to know the cost of this evening for the disciples. Many times he had tried to get them to understand the terrible risk involved in the work of the last few years, but he knew that he had not been heard. In their wildest imaginings they had not envisaged the possibilities that they and he were now facing.

An indication of the intensity of the disciples' anxiety is that not one of them speaks of the fear that is palpable in the room. Occasionally they respond to something Jesus says, but they seem incapable of naming what they dread, as if avoiding it would somehow keep it at bay.

We can discern the emotional undercurrents if we read John's gospel carefully. Intuiting their distress, Jesus deliberately chooses words that are encouraging and comforting. "If it were not so, would I have told you that I go to prepare a place for you?... I will come again ... Where I am, you may be also."

Jesus speaks with gentle repetitiveness, the way a parent might soothe a distressed child. Yet, in spite of this, at least two of the disciples respond sharply, revealing the anger that lies close to the surface. Jesus says, "You know the way to the place where I am going." A quick retort flashes from Thomas. Even though tempered by respect, it directly contradicts Jesus. "Lord, we do not know where you are going! How can we know the way?"

The reply he receives, "I am the way, and the truth, and the life," has become one of the great majestic statements forming the heart of Christian faith, but in that room to that simple man it must have been mystifying. A moment later, as Jesus continues, another of the circle cannot refrain from expressing a sense of mystification. Jesus has just begun to speak of his relationship with the Father when Philip pleads, "Lord, show us the Father, and we will be satisfied"—an indication that he and the others around him are in fact far from satisfied!

The response this time, clear and straightforward, must have been reassuring and strengthening. Jesus says, "Whoever has seen me has seen the Father." There are no further outbursts, no more questions. We cannot tell, but this may have been the moment at which Jesus reaches for the bread and wine to offer the sublime gift we know as eucharist.

As we listen to the voices in the upper room, we realize that we are overhearing exchanges that are possible only because they take place in the context of a mature relationship. It is highly unlikely that such exchanges would have occurred in the sunlit early days under Galilean skies. When we realize this, we also understand something about our own relationship with our Lord and with our Christian faith. Sometimes our having to wrestle with the relationship is itself an indication that it is a maturing one.

While a statement like a creed can give us the illusion that Christian faith is a clear and succinct entity—especially the Apostles' Creed with its precision and brevity—Christianity is also a mysterious and many-faceted edifice. I can recall in student days the late Michael Ramsey of Canterbury saying to us that Christian faith is both story and glory—the story sufficiently simple that it can be told to a child, the glory such that the levels of Christianity cannot be plumbed even by the greatest intellect.

Sometimes we can be distressed when we find ourselves in the deep waters of Christian faith. We may be there because of a book we are reading, or because of something that has happened in our life that has stripped away the seeming simplicity of faith. We may feel aggrieved that Christianity does not allow us the luxury of simplicity. We can feel like Thomas and Philip, exasperated and almost resentful at this God who is proving so elusive.

At such moments we might recall that moment around the table when Jesus looks across at Philip and says clearly and simply, "Whoever has seen me has seen the Father." We might consider this statement as addressed to ourselves, and lay aside the book that has occasioned us exasperation or think again of the event that has forced us to wrestle with our faith. Then we might pick up one of the gospel accounts, turning to an episode—almost any episode—that brings us into the presence of Jesus.

He may be teaching, praying, healing. Whatever he is doing, he has told us that as we watch him, we are watching God. When he speaks to us, we are being spoken to by God. When we are touched by what he says and does and is, we have been touched by God.

❦ EIGHT ❦

Warnings and Reassurances

[Jesus said,] "If the world hates you, be aware that it hated me before it hated you. If you belonged to the world, the world would love you as its own. Because you do not belong to the world, but I have chosen you out of the world—therefore the world hates you.... Whoever hates me hates my Father also. If I had not done among them the works that no one else did, they would not have sin. But now they have seen and hated both me and my Father. It was to fulfill the word that is written in their law, 'They hated me without a cause.' When the Advocate comes, whom I will send to you from the Father, the Spirit of truth who comes from the Father, he will testify on my behalf. You also are to testify because you have been with me from the beginning." (John 15:18–19, 23–27)

Few things can bring about mood changes quicker than tension and stress. This evening's gathering of Jesus with his disciples—the last of many meetings before he is taken and killed—is alive with both tension and stress, especially because no one dares name the reason why.

Because they cannot bring themselves to acknowledge the threat that hangs over them, Jesus is again forced to do what he has attempted countless times in the last few months. He must get them to understand what will soon be demanded of them. But because this reality is so terrifying, and because it threatens everything they desperately cling to, he must also give them reassurance so that they will not disintegrate as individuals and fail to endure as a cohesive group.

Only when he feels he has achieved sufficient reassurance, does he voice the chilling words that need to be said. They will face an unpredictable and dangerous future. A ripple of fear must have spread around the table when they heard him say, "The world hates you." No fewer than eight times during his short explanation does he use the word "hate." He paints vivid images showing the disciples as recipients of violence and rejection.

It is significant—and for our Lord it must have been dispiriting—that his repeated efforts to warn and reassure them produce a familiar response. The previously dammed up tension finally releases in angry rejoinders. They cannot understand what he is saying. "What does he mean ...? ... We do not know what he is talking about." Their irritable exasperation is a pathetic cover for their fear. We hear Jesus change from quiet explaining to urgent pleading, as he tries to make them realize what they will eventually experience. "You will have pain ... But your pain will turn into joy ... You have pain now; but I will see you again ... Your hearts will rejoice ... No one will take your joy from you."

His voice rises as he seeks to grasp this last moment to give them courage for what lies ahead. "I tell you plainly," he pleads. As they force themselves to calm down and listen, he slowly and deliberately presents the heart of what he wants them to know: "I came from the Father and have come into the world; again, I am leaving the world and am going to the Father." Four short and utterly simple statements. There is silence. Will even these words fail to be heard? But a measure of calm descends. Finally someone in the group responds, "Now you are speaking plainly ... we believe that you came from God."

Jesus cannot help but be struck by the irony of it all. It has been hard for them to understand. Even now he knows they have much to learn. He offers them a last reminder of what must be endured, coupled with a word of encouragement: "In the world you face persecution. But take courage; I have conquered the world!"

It is important in the West to remind ourselves that there are many contemporary Christian communities where the stress and tension of this passage—Jesus pleading to be understood and meeting nothing but fearful incomprehension—would be read and identified with in a very immediate way. The terrible scars of Rwanda come to mind, the present agonies of many in Darfur, the siege mentality that is an everyday norm for Christians in parts of Indonesia. To be hated by the world around you, to know persecution, has been a familiar part of Christian experience through history.

We in the Western world may regard this evening conversation in the upper room differently, but it will speak to us nevertheless. We have come to the end of an age when the experience of being hated by the world can remain utterly foreign to us. We have not yet arrived at a stage of being universally hated, but we are beginning to observe a growing mistrust and rejection of Christian faith and institutions. It is not unusual to hear and see occasional expressions of revulsion toward Christian faith and the church.

In such a new reality we need to recall our Lord's warning that such worldly rejection is to be expected. And this rejection may be occasioned partly by the shortcomings of our culture and the church. But perhaps even more important, we need to recall Jesus' assurances that his presence, far from being a memory to be recalled, is a living Holy Spirit, present with us in every age and in spite of cultural change. This is the Spirit from whom we can expect wisdom, guidance, and encouragement to negotiate the new realities in which we must live, pray, worship, and witness.

Perhaps the most important gift we can ask of the Spirit is that our Lord's refusal to hate when hatred was shown toward him may be reflected in our own lives.

❧ NINE ❧

Called into Relationship

[Jesus said,] "I have said these things to you while I am still with you. But the Advocate, the Holy Spirit, whom the Father will send in my name, will teach you everything, and remind you of all that I have said to you. Peace I leave with you; my peace I give to you. I do not give to you as the world gives. Do not let your hearts be troubled, and do not let them be afraid. You heard me say to you, 'I am going away, and I am coming to you.' If you loved me, you would rejoice that I am going to the Father, because the Father is greater than I. And now I have told you this before it occurs, so that when it does occur, you may believe. I will no longer talk much with you, for the ruler of this world is coming. He has no power over me; but I do as the Father has commanded me, so that the world may know that I love the Father. Rise, let us be on our way." (John 14:25–31)

John the Evangelist has allowed us into this last evening of Jesus' physical presence with his disciples as no other writer has done. He has made it possible for us to listen to an intense conversation in which Jesus shares his knowledge with beloved friends, even though he knows it will distress them deeply.

Jesus has spoken of his promise to send the Holy Spirit. Obviously he is making every effort to lessen the disciples' distress at the news that they must face a future without his physical presence. He makes a series of categorical promises. "[The Father] will give you another Advocate ... I will not leave you orphaned ... You will see me; because I live, you also will live."

Jesus then tries to express a truth that completely eludes the circle around the table. He explains that he can claim lordship over a human life only if that life opens itself to him in relationship. "Those who love me," he says, "will be loved by my Father, and I will love them and reveal myself to them." No sooner has he said this but a voice—that of Judas (not Iscariot)—asks a pleading question: "Lord, how is it that you will reveal yourself to us, and not to the world?"

Once again Jesus knows that he has encountered his friends' invincible ability to deny what they cannot accept. There is a hint of resignation in his words: "I have said these things to you while I am still with you. But the Advocate, the Holy Spirit ... will teach you ... and remind you of all that I have said ... I will no longer talk much with you."

At this point in his gospel John tells us something simple but intriguing. Acting apparently on a sudden resolve, Jesus makes the short and almost curt statement, "Rise, let us be on our way." We could be excused for thinking he is tired of trying to make these good, well-meaning, but obtuse men understand. But if this were true, then something happens to change his mind. Did he perhaps look at them and, realizing they were by no means reassured, resign himself to staying longer to offer more encouragement?

For some reason he continues at length. Is it because he has just conceived a vivid and powerful image, one he is almost certain they will understand? "I am the true vine," he says to them. "Just as the branch cannot bear fruit by itself ... neither can you unless you abide in me." Then, in case this is not crystal clear, he adds, " I am the vine, you are the branches."

In a recent BBC interview Karen Armstrong talks about the great emphasis that Western Christianity puts on believing certain propositional truths. She is not the only voice that points to this emphasis.

Armstrong and others are not denying that there are great truths at the heart of Christian faith. They are asking us to remember that we are called to something other than intellectual belief. We are called into nothing less than a loving relationship with God, and as Christians, the way we come to such a relationship is through Jesus. We certainly believe truths about our Lord, truths that indeed make him Lord for us. But our belief in his dying and rising is not a mere acceptance of historical validity, important though this is. The real significance of believing these truths lies in the fact that they call us to a dying to self and a rising to live in relationship with him.

As we listen to John's recalling of that evening in the upper room, we hear Jesus urging his disciples to grasp the true nature of their calling. He has not invited them into an organization. He has called them into a relationship. What the disciples heard in that room is what we, in our better and clearer moments, hear our Lord saying to us. It is in relationship with him that we understand and experience what Christian faith is all about. Just as we cannot know someone else with any intimacy unless a relationship with them begins and grows, so it is for each one of us with our Lord.

The image of the vine and the branches shows us a further truth. By offering this image, Jesus attempts to strengthen not only the bond between himself and his disciples, but also the bonds among all of them. To join with others who have found a relationship to Jesus as Lord—perhaps a congregation in which we feel welcome, or a group among whom we find support—brings us into a rich network of human relationships that can mean much to us in the challenges and successes of our lives.

❦ TEN ❦

Alone with God

Jesus' disciples said, "Yes, now you are speaking plainly, not in any figure of speech! Now we know that you know all things, and do not need to have anyone question you; by this we believe that you came from God." Jesus answered them, "Do you now believe? The hour is coming, indeed it has come, when you will be scattered, each one to his home, and you will leave me alone. Yet I am not alone because the Father is with me. I have said this to you, so that in me you may have peace. In the world you face persecution. But take courage; I have conquered the world!" After Jesus had spoken these words, he looked up to heaven and said, "Father, the hour has come; glorify your Son so that the Son may glorify you." (John 16:29—17:1)

It seems that a point of resolution has been reached between Jesus and his disciples in the room. They have just said they now grasp what he has been trying to make clear to them. "We believe that you came from God." Jesus' reply betrays a hint of sadness, perhaps irony. "Do you now believe?" he says and immediately points to their desertion, which will happen in just a few hours.

None of this seems to matter anymore. Jesus has moved into a kind of detachment. Not that he has in any way rejected them. But he knows that so much is about to happen, and so vast are the issues at stake in the coming struggle, that these faithful simple men cannot grasp it all. There is just one thing left to do before they leave the room and let the terrible sequence of events begin. He decides to pray.

His very first words name two realities. "Father, the hour has come." There is no longer any doubt that time is running out for his earthly ministry, and for his time with these confused and frightened companions on whom the future depends. But before he utters these ominous words, we are reminded of the unbreakable bond between Jesus and his God. Facing a threat all the more chilling because it is still unknown, our Lord names this relationship that has always been precious to him: "Father" is his first word of prayer.

Jesus now adds new meaning to the terror of this moment by repeatedly referring to the coming events as glorious. The term "glory" echoes like a refrain throughout his prayer. It is even applied to his relationship with these very human followers he has gathered. "I have been glorified in them," he says. Then, expressing tender concern for his disciples, Jesus makes it plain that he has no illusions about the future they face. "I ask you to protect them," he prays.

Now Jesus pushes back the horizons of the future to

include "those who will believe in me through their word." For those future millions he prays one thing above all else—unity. Again and again we hear him say the word "one," as if he realizes how difficult such unity will be in the future ages of Christian faith.

We can only imagine the anxious fascination in their faces as the disciples listen to him. They hear him praying for them, then for a future world they cannot begin to imagine. We in turn are awed by this prayer because we know somehow that our Lord is praying also for us.

So much of this prayer points to our Christian vocation and to what is demanded of us by our claim to be his disciples. As our Lord speaks of finishing the work he had been given to do on earth, so we are called to take up the work of God in the world. Jesus makes it plain that Christian faith does not in any sense free us from involvement in the events of our time. Categorically he says of us, "They are in the world ... as you have sent me into the world, so I have sent them into the world."

There are moments in the prayer that should give us pause. Phrases like "protect them" and "guard them" are said more than once. Jesus makes it obvious that living out a Christian vocation in society is far from easy. And yet, precisely at this point, as he hints at serious future challenges, Jesus also names a quality of joyfulness. He prays that "they may have my joy made complete in themselves."

This is an aspect of Christian life we tend to neglect. Serving, believing, obeying, responding—all these things we understand to be our Christian service. But our Lord is asking something more. He seems to be saying that our possessing and communicating a sense of joy in our Christian faith mysteriously completes the joy he knows in his relationship with God. As we reflect on this, we may recall certain people who do indeed communicate joy in their Christian faith, a joy that we sense to be both attractive and contagious.

If we can say that any of this great prayer sounds like pleading, it is when Jesus reflects on the constant struggle for unity in the years ahead—a struggle we know very well in our own time. The terms in which he offers this part of the prayer are significant. At no time does our Lord pray that those who follow him achieve uniformity of belief. He does not envisage a single vast institution. But his deep and even anxious prayer is that those souls who will speak his name in the future, whatever varying forms they may evolve, will also show to the world an essential unity—a oneness of mutual respect, affection, and cooperation.

In the last sentence of his prayer our Lord makes the ultimate demand of us, and the ultimate promise to us. He gives us the reason for everything that has taken place to this point—his coming among us, his sharing of our humanity, his patient fashioning of faith in us, his self-offering that is now imminent.

All is for one thing—that the love he has shown to us may be shown by us to others. This is the ultimate demand. Then the ultimate promise: "I in them." Jesus promises to be within us as grace, making it possible for us in our human loving to show even a faint reflection of his boundless love.

❦ ELEVEN ❦

The Familiar Friend

*Jesus was troubled in spirit, and declared, "Very truly, I tell
you, one of you will betray me." The disciples looked at one
another, uncertain of whom he was speaking. One of his
disciples—the one whom Jesus loved—was reclining next
to him; Simon Peter therefore motioned to him to ask Jesus
of whom he was speaking. So while reclining next to Jesus,
he asked him, "Lord, who is it?" Jesus answered, "It is the
one to whom I give this piece of bread when I have dipped it
in the dish." So when he had dipped the piece of bread, he
gave it to Judas son of Simon Iscariot. After he received the
piece of bread, Satan entered into him. Jesus said to him,
"Do quickly what you are going to do." ... So, after receiv-
ing the piece of bread, he immediately went out. And it was
night. (John 13:21–27, 30)*

O f the many mysteries we encounter in the gospel narrative, none is more resistant to easy solution than the relationship between our Lord and his disciple Judas Iscariot. One reason for this is the paucity of information we have about Judas and his relationship with Jesus. The mystery is compounded by certain moments in the narrative when Jesus shows a clear awareness, not just that he has been betrayed but even who his betrayer is. The most poignant moment occurs as they sit at supper.

Whether by design or happenstance, John and Judas flank Jesus at the table, allowing for the utmost intimacy. Apparently the rest of the group cannot hear every quiet exchange. Finally, when Peter asks John to identify the betrayer, John turns to Jesus and asks the question point-blank. The reply is cryptic: "It is the one to whom I give this piece when I have dipped it." (Sharing food with a special recipient is part of the tradition of the Passover meal.) In the next moment Jesus takes the piece of bread, dips it in the dish, and offers it to Judas with the ambiguous direction, "Do quickly what you are going to do." The real meaning of the words is probably hidden from the rest of the disciples who, most likely, could not even conceive the possibility.

From this moment the events of betrayal take their course. The visit to the authorities. The agreement about when and where the arrest would take place. The pathetic payment that, even in the currency of those days, was merely token and could not possibly have motivated Judas's action.

The question of motivation has always eluded subsequent generations. We will never know if the invitation to be near Jesus and the intimate gesture of dipped bread were a last effort on Jesus' part to bring Judas back into the circle before it was too late. Or was this arrangement Jesus' way of acknowledging that he and Judas were locked in a cosmic drama beyond themselves and had become, to some extent, helpless to change approaching events? All we know is that, at some stage in the next few hours, Judas leads the Jewish authorities to Jesus in Gethsemane, gives his friend a kiss of salutation, and betrays him in the most obvious way.

Theories abound as to what motivated Judas. He was the outsider in the group from the beginning and remained so. He was committed to an understanding of messiah that involved political and even violent action. He wished to force Jesus to act and felt that placing him in danger would have this effect. None of these theories can ever be proved correct, not even by the recent finding and publication of a fourth-century Gnostic Gospel of Judas.

What remains for Christian reflection? Nothing less than the whole mysterious world of human motivation, our own and everyone else's. What motivates us to do anything, even the simplest thing? The answer is not that we are totally unaware but that the motives behind any decision or action are endlessly complex.

One of the roots of the term "to motivate" is the same as the word "motor"—that which drives. We have become increasingly aware of the degree to which our decisions and actions are driven—by our childhood formation, our pressing needs, our fears, our illusions, our loyalties, our convictions, the whole mysterious world of our unconscious. As Christians we are committed to believing ourselves to be creatures with free will. At the same time we know to our cost, through many struggles, how our free will has to wrestle mightily with the forces arraigned against it, each determined to work its will upon us!

This struggle has never been more eloquently expressed than in Paul's intense words in his letter to the community in Rome. "I do not understand my own actions." How often have we said that! "I do not do the good I want, but the evil I do not want is what I do." Paul freely admits that the war raging within him, as desire and conscience, or human will and God's will, grapple constantly with each other. He pleads desperately for understanding and receives insight that, while he can never escape the inner struggle, he possesses in Jesus Christ an ally who, when called on, will fight beside him as he struggles for victory.

Whatever Judas's motivation may have been—conscious or unconscious—everything we know of our Lord Jesus Christ leads us to assume that even Judas was included in the prayer gasped out in agony as the nails pierced. "Father, forgive them; for they do not know what they are doing." Every one of us can be profoundly thankful for that costly absolution of our humanity.

❦ TWELVE ❦

The Garden

*After Jesus had spoken these words, he went out with his
disciples across the Kidron valley to a place where there was
a garden, which he and his disciples entered. Now Judas,
who betrayed him, also knew the place, because Jesus often
met there with his disciples. So Judas brought a detachment
of soldiers together with police from the chief priests and the
Pharisees, and they came there with lanterns and torches
and weapons. Then Jesus, knowing all that was to happen to
him, came forward and asked them, "Whom are you looking
for?" They answered, "Jesus of Nazareth." Jesus replied, "I
am he." Judas, who betrayed him, was standing with them.
(John 18:1–5)*

Somewhere on the way to Gethsemane Jesus pauses, turns to the disciples, and lets them know in stark terms that he expects nothing of them in the hours to come. There will be a future relationship—"after I am raised up, I will go ahead of you to Galilee"—but for the next few hours he expects nothing.

Peter's is the lone voice that challenges Jesus, but in spite of his vehement protesting, Peter takes part in the coming debacle. From now on we see nothing but the deterioration of the relationship between the disciples and their leader. At one point Jesus signals the group to wait, inviting only three of them—Peter, James, and John—to go further with him. After a short walk, even they are pushed away, almost as if Jesus cannot bear human company at this moment.

Because he is fully human, Jesus may sense the possibility of his coming emotional collapse and needed privacy. "I am deeply grieved, even to death," he says before turning and walking among the trees, throwing himself on the ground, and making his desperate plea for some way out of the dreadful death he knew was imminent. Even now he is still prepared to name the intimacy between him and the Father. If the Father wills this death, then the Son will be faithful.

But there is the terrible loneliness. He rises and goes back down the narrow woodland path, only to find the three disciples sleeping. Peter becomes the focus of Jesus' bitterness: "Could you not stay awake with me one hour?" Twice more his longing for solitary prayer and human companionship is acted out. Twice more he finds them asleep. Twice more he says to them—an edge of bitterness in his voice—that the spirit is strong but the flesh is weak. But now we detect a gentleness in his voice: "Are you still sleeping and taking your rest?" And a moment later we hear resignation as it becomes obvious that they are surrounded by those who have been ordered to take him.

The three disciples—the others probably hidden some distance away—watch in horror as Judas emerges from the darkness, kisses Jesus on the cheek, then steps back into the shadows to allow others to detain him and make him prisoner.

"Gethsemane" was the name they called those lower slopes of the mountain. A public place, its paths and clearings must have been used by many. In large noisy cities, such places can be very human zones. They offer solitude, quietness, an easing of stress. There is a chance to converse, to receive and offer advice, to listen to another's private agony or joy, to exchange words of love. We have our own Gethsemanes that offer themselves to us in those moments of life when we seek a refuge.

All of us know how we live between a longing for companionship and a longing for solitariness. It has been said that, while loneliness is the pain of being alone, solitariness is the glory of being alone. Most of us have known both, sometimes ironically experiencing one when we longed for the other. But to be a Christian is to bring yet another element to the constant balancing of solitariness and companionship in our lives.

We are promised a companion even in our solitariness, one who has promised, "I am with you always." These are not just long-ago words of scripture said to a group of fearful believers dreading the loss of someone who has become the centre of their lives. Jesus' prayer, offered for his disciples, pleading that they might always be one, is not only for them but for all Christians. His promise of companionship is for all. Even when we are experiencing and enjoying companionship—where two or three are gathered together—our Lord has promised to be there if we wish to invite his presence.

Perhaps the greatest gift we receive by being allowed to witness our Lord's agony in that garden on the mountainside, is our overhearing his acknowledgement of something we know in our own experience. Addressing three friends who must have been deeply ashamed at their weakness, Jesus says, "The spirit indeed is willing, but the flesh is weak." Because this acknowledgement comes from the depths of his own personal experience, it is for all of us the best of good news. We have his companionship even in our weaknesses and failures. Thanks be to God.

❦ THIRTEEN ❦

The Prisoner

Simon Peter and another disciple followed Jesus. Since that disciple was known to the high priest, he went with Jesus into the courtyard of the high priest, but Peter was standing outside at the gate. So the other disciple, who was known to the high priest, went out, spoke to the woman who guarded the gate, and brought Peter in. The woman said to Peter, "You are not also one of this man's disciples, are you?" He said, "I am not." Now the slaves and the police had made a charcoal fire because it was cold, and they were standing around it and warming themselves. Peter also was standing with them and warming himself. (John 18:15–18)

Taking the prisoner is a clandestine operation carried out after dark to avoid the possibility of a public outcry in his support. A nighttime capture also precludes any disturbance of the peace, which would alienate the Roman administration and make conviction and sentencing more difficult to attain.

There is a brief scuffle, probably because of the need to leave the area swiftly. In a momentary exchange Jesus ridicules his captors, citing their inability to take him publicly on one of the many occasions when he preached to the crowds. Peter lashes out and wounds one of the guards, only to be reprimanded by Jesus, who tends to the injured man. Then they begin the long climb up the slope to the house of Caiaphas. There the beating and questioning begin.

Witnesses are produced, but none of them provides sufficient evidence to carry charges that might stand in a Roman court. At last two testify to hearing Jesus say that he would destroy the temple and build it again in three days. However insane this claim sounds, it can be offered to nervous Roman officialdom as a threat to public order. For Jewish ears, Jesus' oblique response to Caiaphas's command, "Tell us if you are the Messiah, the Son of God," can count as blasphemy. The insults and beatings continue.

Meanwhile Peter waits, surrounded by strangers, exhausted by the hour and the events of this terrible night, huddled by the fire, desperately keeping as low a profile as possible, hoping that somehow all this will pass. Twice his cover is nearly lifted—first by a woman, later by two men in quick succession. To the last probe Peter's northern accent belies his denial. Fearful of capture, devastated by having to deny Jesus to survive, Peter leaves the fire and moves out into the approaching dawn. As he does so, Jesus emerges under guard, evidence of physical abuse clearly visible. For a moment their eyes meet. Peter's world collapses in remorse.

A hastily convened meeting called by Caiaphas decides to present the prisoner to the procurator. Having followed Jesus into the risky confines of Caiaphas's chambers, it is unlikely that Peter would have left the vicinity. He is probably watching as a security detachment, accompanied by various officials, sets out for Pilate's headquarters in the Antonine Tower overlooking the temple area. Shackled, bruised, exhausted from lack of sleep, Jesus walks in their midst.

We who read these events as sacred scripture are witnessing how our human nature negotiates those moments in life when crisis strikes. We are not only watching our Lord cope with being confronted by a dreadful ordeal; we are also seeing his friends, especially Peter, dealing with a shattering world in which they had hoped for much and given absolute trust to one whom they naturally called Master.

All of us live in some kind of self-constructed story. When life shatters our assumptions about the world and ourselves, suddenly bringing us to crisis—illness or pain or great loss—we are forced to discover what resources we have to respond and survive.

Here we see various responses to a terrifying situation. Most flee, unable or unwilling to face the situation. Faithfulness is lost. Survival is paramount. Many of us have known disappointment in what we thought were firm and trustworthy friendships. Suddenly those whom we expected to be there for us in our need are not there. In spite of our deep hurt, all we can do is try to understand the possible reasons for betrayal.

Peter's response is different. He attempts to remain

faithful in spite of everything—his own fears, his inability to understand what is happening. We have all experienced this kind of response in life's grim times. We ourselves may have reacted this way or been deeply grateful for this reaction in a friend.

Our Lord's way is different again. To follow him means that we fully embrace the terror of the moment, acknowledge its grim reality, even risk being overcome by it, then move through the depths of human suffering to the realization that we are not alone, that there is a source of strength beyond ourselves, that we are in the arms of a loving and gracious God.

❦ FOURTEEN ❦

The Weakness of Power

Pilate entered the headquarters again, summoned Jesus, and asked him, "Are you the King of the Jews?" Jesus answered, "Do you ask this on your own, or did others tell you about me?" Pilate replied, "I am not a Jew, am I? Your own nation and the chief priests have handed you over to me. What have you done?" Jesus answered, "My kingdom is not from this world. If my kingdom were from this world, my followers would be fighting to keep me from being handed over to the Jews. But as it is, my kingdom is not from here." Pilate asked him, "So you are a king?" Jesus answered, "You say that I am a king. For this I was born, and for this I came into the world, to testify to the truth. Everyone who belongs to the truth listens to my voice." Pilate asked him, "What is truth?" (John 18:33–38)

There may have been some hours' interval between the first round of brutal interrogation in Caiaphas's house and the subsequent decision to take the prisoner to the procurator. This decision seems to have been made in the early hours of Friday morning. Thought would have been given, and information obtained, about the shape of the procurator's day. A sympathetic verdict could depend on Pilate's mood. To irritate him by presenting the case too early would be foolish. To delay too long would lessen the chance of a satisfactory resolution.

The first encounter with Roman authority ends inconclusively. In all the gospel narratives it becomes obvious that Pilate is wary. Even the contrived and sanctimonious form of the charges, framed in political rather than religious terms, fails to get a quick decision. "We found this man perverting our nation, forbidding us to pay taxes to the emperor."

Pilate sees through the device. He does not react as hoped for. Instead, a passing mention of Galilee gives him a chance to prevaricate. With any luck Herod might deal with the troublemaker. The act of referring the prisoner is a signal to Herod that he can have *carte blanche* to deal as he wishes and the Roman administration will look the other way. Pilate gives an order and Jesus is hustled through the still dark streets.

Herod, decadent and always devious, is far too good a politician to take the bait. He contemptuously dismisses Jesus and sends the frustrated Jewish delegation back to Pilate with their prisoner. The latter now declares himself. As far as he is concerned, there is no cause to condemn. He makes a last effort to derail the conspiracy. Jewish custom at the Passover allows him to release a prisoner—this quiet northern rabbi or a tough radicalized terrorist named Barabbas. Pilate announces the alternatives, but voices in the crowd are adamant. Nothing but death will satisfy.

Pilate's last question is full of frustrated sarcasm. "Shall I crucify your King?" The reply that swells up toward him is politically lethal, and he knows it. "We have no king but the emperor." Years later John will point to this moment as the end of Pilate's resistance when he writes, "He handed him over to them to be crucified."

To watch while a public figure disintegrates is not a pretty sight. Pontius Pilate, procurator of Judea, representative of imperial Roman power, possessing final authority over every human life in his assigned territory, is not the first to discover that even great political power can find itself manipulated into a situation where it has become chillingly vulnerable. Through the eyes of the gospel writers we watch as someone in a position of power is drawn into a course of action, which he himself regrets, but before which he finds himself helpless.

Hardly a day goes by that men and women do not have such experiences in the unrelenting demands and complexities of professional life, particularly in business and politics.

If we are prepared to be honest, we can find a double standard at work in such situations. When we are forced to make decisions that are morally ambiguous—sometimes even morally reprehensible—we are quick to defend our actions. We claim to have done all that could reasonably be expected of us. We point to the complex issues that needed to inform our decision. We cite the deviousness and unreasonableness of others, which have forced us to act as we have done.

But when we hear or read of such decisions in the life of public figures, we are quick to condemn. We point to a lack of moral courage. We enumerate the many alternatives that could have been chosen. We demand a level of integrity that we probably never have had to rise to! At such times we indulge in psychological projection, condemning in others the moral compromising we are not prepared to acknowledge in ourselves.

Jesus was extraordinarily blunt in his contempt for this kind of behaviour. He spoke of the ease with which we identify a minor fault in another, while at the same moment ignoring a major fault in ourselves. "Why," he asked acidly, "do you see the speck in your neighbour's eye, but do not notice the log in your own eye?"

A clear awareness of these realities in human nature enables us not only to refrain from easy dismissal of the personal and professional struggles of other people, but also to be rigorously honest with ourselves when we face decisions that allow no perfect resolution. Even if our moral struggles have involved much lesser matters, all of us have sat in Pilate's seat.

❦ FIFTEEN ❦

The Tormenting

*Then they all shouted out together, "Away with this fellow!
Release Barabbas for us!" (This was a man who had been put
in prison for an insurrection that had taken place in the city,
and for murder.) Pilate, wanting to release Jesus, addressed
them again; but they kept shouting, "Crucify, crucify him!"
A third time he said to them, "Why, what evil has he done?
I have found in him no ground for the sentence of death; I
will therefore have him flogged and then release him." But
they kept urgently demanding with loud shouts that he should
be crucified; and their voices prevailed. So Pilate gave his
verdict that their demand should be granted. He released
the man they asked for, the one who had been put in prison
for insurrection and murder, and he handed Jesus over as
they wished.* (Luke 23:18–25)

There is something chilling about the phrase, "He [Pilate] handed Jesus over as they wished." Matthew and Mark are more precise. They tell us, "He handed [Jesus] over to be crucified." Luke's lack of the specific "to be crucified," suggests that anything is possible now. Even the pretense of the law's protection has been withdrawn.

"Their wishes" are rapidly revealed. What takes place next is brutal and sadistic, a grim display of gratuitous violence. We are seeing what inevitably develops in all zones of war and occupation—the brutalization of human beings who previously may have lived by reasonably civilized mores. The gospel writers describe this particular scene of our Lord's suffering in words. Today we see it again and again in searing media images.

Earlier translations of scripture make the improbable statement that a whole battalion assembled around Jesus. It is highly unlikely that a thousand men were involved. During feast days the army would have been preoccupied with preserving security throughout the city. The word "cohort," used in the new translation, gives a more likely picture of the reality we are witnessing.

The gospel narrative becomes precise and unsparing at this point, almost as if every moment has been scorched into the memory of a witness who later conveyed the scene to members of the early Christian community. There is a harsh rough sound to the language used to describe this horrible interlude, even to the phrase, "twisting some thorns into a crown, they put it on his head." The images flash quickly before our eyes. They strip him ... put on a scarlet robe ... a crown of thorns ... a reed in his hand ... they mock ... they spit ... they strike him on the head—all with the brutality of men themselves brutalized by countless such scenes.

Our Lord's physical suffering haunted the early church.

The Gospel of Peter, a third-century document, is even more specific about these terrible hours. "Having taken the Lord, they pushed him as they ran and said, 'Let us drag around the Son of God now that we have power over him.' And they put a purple robe on him and made him sit on the seat of judgment, saying, 'Judge justly, king of Israel.' And one of them brought a crown of thorns and put it on the Lord's head; and others stood and spat in his eyes, and still others slapped his cheeks; others pricked him with a reed, and some scourged him, saying, 'With this honour let us honour the Son of God.' "

One afternoon in November 1895 Oscar Wilde was released from Reading Jail. Handcuffed and still in prison clothing, he was forced to stand for half an hour on the platform at Clapham Junction where a crowd gathered to laugh and jeer at him. One man who recognized Wilde spat in his face. Some time later Wilde wrote, "For a year after that was done to me, I wept every day at the same hour and for the same space of time."

That simple and heart-rending statement points to something easily forgotten—the mental and spiritual torture that can accompany physical suffering, especially when the pain is inflicted as an expression of hatred or contempt. This must have been true of our Lord's experience during the hours when he was at the mercy of that army unit, its members probably bored and eager for diversion.

We see this behaviour in the conflicts of our own time, most recently in Bosnia, Somalia, and Iraq. The restraints on human nature seem to snap, and men and women almost vie with one another to conceive and demonstrate the greatest cruelty that can be devised.

Most of us are unlikely to find ourselves in positions where we can, or even would wish to, inflict physical suffering on another. Yet the battlefield is not the only arena where pain can be inflicted. The silent cruelty to vulnerable elderly people in a nursing home. The remembered abuse or punishment in a Residential School. Any place where there is dependence, vulnerability, and helplessness—even considering the innumerable kindnesses done, and the tender care given, in such situations.

Professional life can become an arena for mental and spiritual suffering when power takes advantage of weakness, or when dislike or even contempt sours a relationship, making communication severely hurtful.

As we look upon our Lord's physical suffering, we are reminded of our own capacity to speak and act in ways deeply wounding to others who, for many reasons, may be in no position to escape our animosities. But precisely because we regard Jesus as our Lord, we have in him a source of grace for our efforts to transform such hatreds into acceptance of, and respect for, the humanity of those around us.

❧ SIXTEEN ❧

The Journey

As they led [Jesus] away, they seized a man, Simon of Cyrene, who was coming from the country, and they laid the cross on him, and made him carry it behind Jesus. A great number of the people followed him, and among them were women who were beating their breasts and wailing for him. … When they came to the place that is called The Skull, they crucified Jesus there with the criminals, one on his right and one on his left. (Luke 23:26–27, 33)

It may have been obvious from the beginning of the procession that Jesus was incapable of carrying the heavy wooden beam that would eventually bear the weight of his hanging body. Almost all his energy would have been sapped by the vicious beating.

The procession probably set out from the Citadel, which today still stands beside one of the main gates to the city, the Jaffa gate. It is not unlikely that Simon, newly arrived in a ship just docked from Cyrenia, would have been pulled from the stream of visitors early in the proceedings, certainly to his astonishment and probably to his absolute terror. Being forced to participate in a crucifixion at the orders of the Roman authorities probably made him fear greatly for his own life.

This journey to the killing place was not long, at the most three or four modern blocks to the western edge of the city. The pathetic procession, made public to intimidate the population in general, would have had to force its way through narrow alleys crowded with people hurrying on Friday afternoon to shop for groceries before sundown and the sabbath. Some would have been oblivious to yet another Roman crucifixion, some would have been curious, many would have resented the inconvenience to their various domestic and family preoccupations.

At some stage another group joins the procession. Two petty thieves are destined also for execution. This addition would have been of no great consequence. The sight was familiar, almost routine. Jesus may have become aware of familiar voices, perhaps even faces. He tries to warn those friendly to him that the brutalized and corrupt society to which he has become victim cannot last for long without collapse. "The days are surely coming when they will say ... to the mountains, 'Fall on us!' and to the hills, 'Cover us!'"

So frequent were crucifixions that the uprights were often

already in place. But sometimes the heavy crossbeam would be fitted into the upright while still on the ground. Then, if the squad were for some reason prepared to be as merciful as possible, the prisoner would be forced quickly on to the beam, his arms and legs held until the dreadful spikes were hammered firmly into the wood, and the whole obscene engine of torture hauled to a vertical position until it crashed into the waiting hole and the hours of unimaginable agony began.

"We may not know, we cannot tell, what pains he had to bear," wrote Cecil Alexander in her hymn, "There is a green hill far away."

One day in Jerusalem, walking in our Lord's footsteps, jostled in alleyways as crowded now as then, I was struck by the shortness of that terrible journey. I realized I should have known this, for he could not possibly have endured a long journey to his death. The significance of his journey brought to mind the brief journey I myself have made on innumerable occasions to another raised area, another place of sacrifice. I have left my pew and walked forward to the altar to receive the bread and wine, the sacrament available to me only because of the original self-giving of Jesus.

Today in Jerusalem, you can leave the Citadel close by the Jaffa Gate and wend your way through the narrow alleys to arrive at the Church of the Holy Sepulchre—its Eastern name, the Church of the Resurrection. You can enter through the huge doors, turn right, ascend a flight of stone steps, and find yourself in a small chapel. Moving a few steps forward you can see beneath the gleaming candled altar a small opening in the floor. If you kneel—and who could not kneel—you can place a hand on the hard cold rock that in one of the church's most ancient traditions is the ground of Calvary itself.

On reaching my church, I realized that only about fifteen minutes had passed since I set out. I had walked just a few blocks—without effort, with little physical exertion. I was moved to consider the comparative length of our Lord's journey on that long-ago day—the agony of each step, the dread of the destination. As I reached down to touch the hard rock, I realized how often I had almost casually reached for the bread of his broken body in eucharist.

Never after that day have I walked the short journey to the parish or cathedral altar without recalling his journey. And never have I taken the bread of his body without recalling the cost of its terrible breaking, freely paid.

❦ SEVENTEEN ❦

I Am Thirsty

Meanwhile, standing near the cross of Jesus were his mother, and his mother's sister, Mary the wife of Clopas, and Mary Magdalene. When Jesus saw his mother and the disciple whom he loved standing beside her, he said to his mother, "Woman, here is your son." Then he said to the disciple, "Here is your mother." And from that hour the disciple took her into his own home. After this, when Jesus knew that all was now finished, he said (in order to fulfill the scripture), "I am thirsty." A jar full of sour wine was standing there. So they put a sponge full of the wine on a branch of hyssop and held it to his mouth. When Jesus had received the wine, he said, "It is finished." Then he bowed his head and gave up his spirit. (John 19:25–30)

As we discern different nuances in the four accounts of our Lord's crucifixion, we see and hear a succession of faces and voices. There are moments when it would seem that, in spite of the hideous pain, Jesus was to some degree aware of those around him.

Looking at the faces and listening to the voices present during the earlier stages of the execution—whether of idle bystanders, exultant temple officials, or unfortunate ones hanging on nearby crosses—we encounter only jeering, hatred, and contempt. The solitary exception is the condemned felon beside Jesus. In replying to him Jesus shows that he is at least partially conscious.

At a later stage in the interminable noonday hours, the voices change. Perhaps the terrible cry of desolation that suddenly escapes from the dying man induces a sense of awe, even in the curiosity seekers. "My God, my God, why have you forsaken me?" Someone is moved to respond, lifting to Jesus' lips a wet sponge that is refused, perhaps because he is only dimly aware of the gesture.

At some moment in his agony Jesus becomes aware of loving faces looking up at him. The inexpressibly precious gift of love at such a time gives him the energy to focus momentarily on a situation long unresolved. The relationship between his mother and himself has known its painful moments of hurt and misunderstanding. Now, seeing her beside his friend John, he commends her to the disciple's care.

As if this moment of consciousness has awakened agonizing thirst, Jesus asks for a drink. Again a drenched sponge is lifted to his mouth. For a moment tongue and lips and throat are bathed; then life begins to ebb away. There is a last whisper of surrender. Because it is John alone who records the words, "It is finished," we may surmise that his final act of discipleship may have been to proffer the wine-soaked sponge to his Master and to be near enough to the foot of the cross to hear those last words.

So much is retained from my childhood. A legend. Nearly half a millennia before Patrick set foot in Ireland, the high king of Ireland looked at a sky inexplicably darkening long before noon. Terrified he called his chief druid and asked the meaning of this fearful portent. The druid answered, "O king, this darkness tells of the dying of a high king even greater than you, for he rules even over death." In this way the mingled majesty, terror, and hope of Jesus' crucifixion and resurrection were communicated to a child.

In later years that child would arrive at an understanding of other moments in those terrible hours. As an adult he would read the cry, "Why have you forsaken me," and recognize it as the cry of so many souls who have known great suffering and loss. As a priest he would point those men and women to the cry of their Lord who, because he echoes their desolation, becomes their companion in suffering and, therefore, their source of grace.

As a priest he would encounter men and women carrying various degrees of guilt about their relationship with aging parents. For such people he would recall the moment when Jesus looks down from the cross and sees through a haze of pain and nausea the face of his mother. Memories, however momentary, must have come—encounters remembered when she was neglected, even at times dismissed, by his impatient and all-consuming vision of the kingdom of God. Now, as he pays the terrible price exacted by that vision, he takes what is almost the last moment of life to express a loving care for his mother. Such an insight of scripture can transform guilt about a parental relationship into either understanding of past failures or, if time remains, loving action in the present.

Perhaps most poignant is the difficulty many have in sharing themselves even with an old friend who is dying. We feel we will not know what to say or do. When we summon the courage to make such a visit, we discover it is not about saying or doing so much as about being—just being there. If there is to be any doing, it is of utterly simple things—offering a tissue, fluffing a pillow, touching an outstretched arm, raising or lowering a bed that has become uncomfortable, listening to the memory of a moment once shared.

All such moments and simple kindnesses take on a shining significance when we understand them to be, in a small way, a reflection of the caring human response made to Jesus' hoarse plea, "I am thirsty."

❦ EIGHTEEN ❦

A Costly Friendship

After these things, Joseph of Arimathea, who was a disciple of Jesus, though a secret one because of his fear of the Jews, asked Pilate to let him take away the body of Jesus. Pilate gave him permission; so he came and removed his body. Nicodemus, who had at first come to Jesus by night, also came, bringing a mixture of myrrh and aloes, weighing about a hundred pounds. They took the body of Jesus and wrapped it with the spices in linen cloths, according to the burial custom of the Jews. Now there was a garden in the place where he was crucified, and in the garden there was a new tomb in which no one had ever been laid. And so, because it was the Jewish day of Preparation, and the tomb was nearby, they laid Jesus there. (John 19:38–42)

In any age and society most people hesitate to become involved with the law, particularly its criminal aspects. Any possibility of guilt by association—common in some societies—is extremely dangerous.

We need to remember this as we watch what happens late on the afternoon of the first Good Friday. Immediately after Jesus takes his last breath on the cross, all the gospel writers introduce us to two men. One of them, Nicodemus, we met fleetingly when he engaged Jesus in conversation. The other, Joseph, we observed as a silent participant in a recent meeting of the Sanhedrin.

On the occasion in question, the Sanhedrin has assembled to deal with the increasing threat to public order coming from Jesus' ministry. Both Nicodemus and Joseph occupy seats in this very powerful group. It is not yet widely known that the rabbi from Nazareth has become significant in both their lives.

These two men now face a situation that, unless they are careful, could seriously damage their public positions. They are associated with a known criminal, a threat to the state. Nicodemus takes a great risk by protesting the agenda of the meeting as outside the due process of law. He gets a curt, sarcastic, and even threatening official response, which strongly hints that his new loyalty may be known in high places. "Surely you are not also from Galilee, are you?" Elsewhere in the circle Joseph decides to remain silent.

But now that the tragic sequence has been played out and there is a corpse hanging in the sun, Joseph decides to act. He has much to lose. He could leave the city and keep a low profile in his villa on the western slopes of the province. He must have been tempted, but he decides to risk everything. In the gospel, Mark notes that Joseph went "boldly" to Pilate, suggesting that there was at least some danger involved. Joseph is given permission to take the rabbi's body.

Joseph's next act indicates a friendship already formed with Nicodemus. He invites the latter's assistance. Together—and likely with other help—they jeopardize their positions and take down the brutalized body from the cross.

In the apocryphal Gospel of Peter there is a beautiful passage that describes these moments under the late afternoon sun of that day. "Then they drew out the nails from the hands of the Lord and laid him upon the earth. And the whole earth was shaken and there came a great fear. Then the sun shone and it was found to be the ninth hour ... And he took the Lord and washed him, and wrapped him in a linen shroud, and brought him to his own tomb, called the garden of Joseph."

We can assume that both men noted and welcomed the presence of two women who watched from a short distance away.

Helder Camara, for many years Bishop of Recife in Brazil, an immensely courageous challenger of social injustices, once remarked that "the real revolutionaries are the rich who are ready to act for justice."

In the loyalty and commitment shown by Nicodemus and Joseph, we see something of the challenge people face when they endanger their position in society by acting as their conscience dictates. In tending to their friend's body, both men risked a great deal. They could have chosen otherwise—Nicodemus to keep silent, Joseph to retire to his western property. Yet neither could make such a choice and live with himself.

In 1833 the English Parliament passed the Slavery Abolition Act. One month before that historic day William

Wilberforce died. For most of his political life he had expended tremendous energy in his bid to bring forward that legislation. Many had worked with him, including the Quaker community, but it was Wilberforce's social position, money, and influence that made the difference in the struggle, one that was costly for Wilberforce in many ways.

Ironically, it can be very difficult for the affluent and powerful to champion such a decision. To act in any society, our own included, in the name of justice always carries some risk. Powerful forces can oppose any policy that threatens the status quo. Long and valued friendships may be strained, even lost. Family life can suffer from vicious public attack. Some members of the family may fail to share the vision of justice and reform that energizes another family member.

When his friend and government colleague from Arimathea asked for help in the sad duty that called them to respond, Nicodemus may have recalled the conversation he had had with the rabbi long before Jesus became a focus of the forces that destroyed him. Perhaps Nicodemus remembered a quiet voice saying to him, "The wind blows where it chooses, and you hear the sound of it, but you do not know where it comes from or where it goes. So it is with everyone who is born of the Spirit."

Nicodemus and Joseph are not the only people in positions of power who have discovered that the call of justice sometimes comes in the words or the voice of the rabbi from Nazareth, demanding a response that does not count the cost.

❦ NINETEEN ❦

The Waiting Time

It was the day of Preparation, and the sabbath was beginning. The women who had come with him from Galilee followed, and they saw the tomb and how his body was laid. Then they returned, and prepared spices and ointments. (Luke 23:54–56)

The Canadian poet Lorna Fowler has written lines she calls "The Middle Time." She is thinking of those phases in life that are neither beginnings nor endings but the time in between. She refers to such phases as "the middle time/of enduring, changing, trying/despairing, continuing, becoming."

Those words might well describe what happened during the long sabbath hours that followed the death of Jesus. We have almost nothing recorded from those hours, with the exception of a single sentence. Luke tells us about a group of women from Galilee—he does not name them—who carefully looked to see where and how Jesus' body had been laid, presumably by Joseph and Nicodemus and perhaps a few others courageous enough to assist. Luke says that these women prepared spices and ointments just before the sabbath began. But then, "On the sabbath they rested according to the commandment."

We can assume that Joseph and Nicodemus did likewise, perhaps in Nicodemus's residence. It is not unlikely that Joseph, his own home halfway to the coast, would have accepted his colleague's invitation to stay and share the sabbath as a guest.

What of the others? For most of them, especially those who some days before had come south from Galilee with Jesus, the city would have been a strange place—unfamiliar, inhospitable, and now, in view of their association with a convicted and executed felon, dangerous. They would have searched for safe houses where local people might have been prepared to offer hospitality out of a common interest in Jesus' ministry.

We can imagine their feelings and at least some of their responses. They would, of course, feel desolation and sorrow at the death of a friend, coupled with horror at the way in which he had died. Some might suffer shame and regret at the way they had failed to support him, even though they were helpless in the face of the forces ranged against them.

Many ordinary things needed doing when the hours of sabbath ended. Groceries had to be bought for hosts and guests. The whereabouts of friends had to be ascertained, if they had not made contact since the fearful scattering in the darkness of Gethsemane. From the evidence of the gospels, it would seem that gradually many gathered in the same place, almost as if they were instinctively seeking reassurance and security in solidarity.

It would be easy—and quite wrong—to imagine these men and women spending those hours in rapt anticipation of the unbelievable news they would soon receive. Someone has observed that, of all the Christian generations, only they knew the deep desolation that lies between crucifixion and resurrection.

All of us have known times of waiting, from the most casual, when nothing more than the arrival of an expected airplane is involved, or the slow progression of a line-up at a bank counter, to those times when nothing less than the rest of our life may be affected. Even if the interval is actually short, the result of a medical test can take an eternity to arrive, especially if we are worried about a specific symptom.

All of us have our ways of dealing with such waiting times. We may express frustration and even anger, feeling resentment that we are being robbed of precious minutes or hours to do the thousand things that constantly beckon and demand. If we must wait for something we either long for or dread—the response from a beloved, or a verdict perhaps legal or medical—we are almost helpless against the anxiety. We can swing from confidence to terror, and find ourselves emotionally exhausted. Sometimes if we are fortunate, we will sleep, only to wake to the realization that we still must wait.

Christian faith cannot shield us from the cost of such times, as it cannot shield us from what Hamlet calls "the slings and arrows of outrageous fortune." But Christianity offers us resources that, while they cannot remove the pain of loss or suffering, can enable us to find grace and strength to grapple with what must be borne. Being Christian, and having a Christian community in which to share loss and pain, can at times make all the difference between personal disintegration and the strengthening of resolve.

On the first Easter Saturday—as we would call that day—those shocked men and women must have known many responses to their terrible loss. Some would have been desolate, others stoical. Some would have displayed strong emotion, others deep silence. Some would have tried to give comfort to their friends, others to find comfort in their circle of faith.

In these things nothing changes. The mysteries of human nature and experience remain. Yet we possess a gift denied to those early followers and friends. We know today that, in our times of waiting and hoping, we are loved and cared for by One who moved beyond pain, beyond even death, to new life.

❦ TWENTY ❦

The Question

The next day, that is, after the day of Preparation, the chief priests and the Pharisees gathered before Pilate and said, "Sir, we remember what that impostor said while he was still alive, 'After three days I will rise again.' Therefore command the tomb to be made secure until the third day; otherwise his disciples may go and steal him away, and tell the people, 'He has been raised from the dead,' and the last deception would be worse than the first." Pilate said to them, "You have a guard of soldiers; go, make it as secure as you can." So they went with the guard and made the tomb secure by sealing the stone. (Matthew 27:62–66)

It was not enough that the troublesome prophet had been eliminated. His cross, and the crosses of the two petty criminals, now stood empty during the morning hours of the sabbath in a city stilled by religious observation. But it took more than religious piety to impede the demands of political necessity.

Sometime in those early hours a quiet meeting took place, most likely in the offices or home of Caiaphas the high priest. The Galilean nuisance may have been satisfactorily dealt with, but a completely secure outcome was not yet assured. There was still the possibility of isolated disturbances and general social unrest. Although the trial had been manipulated to bring about the desired outcome, it remained true that the Galilean had collected a substantial following. That following, which existed predominantly in the north of the country, was still capable of fomenting resistance. Even here in the capital, while the central core of the movement seemed to have dispersed, it was not known whether they could make more trouble. Steps had to be taken to avoid unrest.

It was reasonable for the Roman administration to think that killing the main actor would deal adequately with the crisis. They simply did not understand the power of religious fervour. The high priest and his circle were under no such illusions, and so the quiet meeting took place sometime in the morning hours.

When the decision had been taken to approach the procurator once more, the delegation was formed and moved through the quiet city to the residence. They were under no illusion that they would be welcome guests, even for a short audience. The high priest knew his man: they had crossed paths more than once, usually to Pilate's disadvantage. Caiaphas knew that the procurator would still be stinging from the public way he had been manipulated into cooperation. This approach would need to be carefully handled.

Matthew's text communicates the care of the approach while retaining the slight note of threat. Since the impostor had been heard to make a ridiculous claim to rise from the dead within three days of his execution, would it not be wise to forestall the likelihood of his body being taken and the wild claim being strengthened? If this were to happen, the ensuing disturbances would perhaps be worse than what had just been prevented. "The last deception would be worse than the first." Again Pilate is subtly reminded that the one danger to his position is the outbreak of social unrest.

Pilate's brusque response stops short of a contemptuous dismissal. "You have a guard of soldiers; go, make it as secure as you can." His last words clearly convey his low opinion of the temple police. Ironically, the decision of the delegation to go to the tomb with its own security detachment—as Matthew tells us—reflects the same lack of confidence.

The inclusion of this brief episode shows us that, while the hours following the sabbath may seem to have been uneventful in terms of the stricken community, they were by no means uneventful in other ways. The request made to Pilate is a tribute to how seriously the temple authorities were concerned about Jesus and his popular support.

Two communities were reacting to Jesus' death. The community of those nearest to him, for whom he had come to mean everything, were dismayed, even traumatized, by what was for them absolute tragedy. The other community, though buoyed by the success of their efforts to destroy Jesus, still felt him to be a threat, even in death.

As we look at these two communities responding to Jesus' death, a question is begged of us. How do we ourselves regard his death? We are, of course, in a very different position from those long-ago men and women—we know the triumph that is to come. But this does not release us from the necessity of voicing our attitude to this death. We need to come to terms with its meaning for our own lives, in the same fashion as Cecil Alexander tried to do for herself when she wrote the deceptively simple lines, "He died that we might be forgiven /He died to make us good."

What is my response? Even as I begin to write, I know that words will fail. I believe that Jesus shared in all ways my human nature, that he lifted that nature, as I can never do, to a level of absolute self-offering and obedience to the will of the One he always called Father. Jesus did this even at the cost of life itself. I believe that, when Jesus did this, he also lifted my human nature with his own to that same Father, making me worthy in a way that I could never attain on my own, and for which I am grateful beyond words. In response to this ultimate act of love, I try, knowing that I will fail, to live my life so that, in spite of my failures, I will be found in some way worthy of Jesus' gift to me.

On that long-ago Saturday—to use our name for that day—men and women tried to come to terms with Jesus' death in different ways and for different reasons. Perhaps the best way we can use these hours, lit for us by the anticipation of resurrection, is to ask ourselves the question, "What does the death of Jesus mean for me?"

TWENTY-ONE

The First Day of the Week

But Mary stood weeping outside the tomb. As she wept, she bent over to look into the tomb; and she saw two angels in white, sitting where the body of Jesus had been lying, one at the head and the other at the feet. They said to her, "Woman, why are you weeping?" She said to them, "They have taken away my Lord, and I do not know where they have laid him." When she had said this, she turned around and saw Jesus standing there, but she did not know that it was Jesus. Jesus said to her, "Woman, why are you weeping? Whom are you looking for?" Supposing him to be the gardener, she said to him, "Sir, if you have carried him away, tell me where you have laid him, and I will take him away." Jesus said to her, "Mary!" She turned and said to him in Hebrew, "Rabbouni!" (which means Teacher).
(John 20:11–16)

Before consciousness finally slips away, Jesus is able to recognize two faces looking up at him in an agony of helplessness. With almost incomprehensible resolve his mother, supported by his friend John, stands below her son's terrible imprisoning. Perhaps a hoarse whisper from the cross draws them nearer. Summoning what remains of his strength, Jesus commends his mother to the care of his friend and disciple.

Whether our Lord's ability to see people at this stage of his dying is severely limited, we do not know. We are aware that three women stood at that moment below his cross. The second was his aunt, his mother's sister, Mary the wife of Clopas, who had already shown immense faithfulness to him and his ministry. The third was Mary of Magdala.

A reading of the gospels will show us this woman gradually moving nearer to the killing ground. She is among a group of women who "had come with Jesus from Galilee," and who watched carefully "from afar" as Joseph of Arimathea and his Sanhedrin colleague Nicodemus placed Jesus' body in Joseph's new tomb. Later, having returned to their lodgings, the women planned. They would let the rest of the sabbath hours go by, try to get a night's rest, and then gather the various traditional resources needed to tend the body—though it is interesting and moving that Nicodemus had himself spent a considerable amount of money on spices and linen for Jesus' body.

In the dawn of the first day of the week—our Sunday morning—the women set out. The world would again be bustling and busy—shops open, carts rumbling on cobbles. Few would notice a small group of women. Even if they were seen and their destination known, the authorities would welcome their actions as acknowledgment and public confirmation of Jesus' death.

This group of women, of whom Mary of Magdala is one,

is met by the sight of the stone rolled away. They are given a ringing announcement that Jesus is risen. Stunned, understandably perplexed, even frightened, they return to tell the others. They are received with absolute disbelief.

Perhaps this disbelief forges Mary of Magdala's determination to be absolutely sure of what she has experienced. Returning by herself she finds the tomb empty. This time there is no ringing announcement. She is alone in the pre-dawn shadows. Distraught, she returns to the community and tells them of the empty tomb. Possibly because this information is practical and can be investigated, the men are galvanized into response. With Mary, Peter and John go to the tomb, and each in his own way is awed by the implications of what he sees.

Peter and John have hardly left when Mary has the encounter that will change her life forever. Hearing herself named by a familiar and loved voice, she recognizes Jesus clearly. Transported with joy, she runs to where she knows the friends are gathered, and becomes the first voice to announce his resurrection to all Christian generations to come.

In this dawn-light journey, Mary of Magdala's experience becomes the experience of every Christian. She and we seek for Jesus as our risen and living lord. In this seeking, there are times of pain and loss and helplessness. There are times— sometimes even long periods—of spiritual emptiness. Most of us move between times of a strong sense of our Lord's presence and times of feeling that he is absent from us. As with any human relationship, the quality ebbs and flows. To be aware that our connection with the holy is a relationship rather than an intellectual believing or not believing, can help us deal with this changing quality of spiritual experience.

We are never more at one with Mary of Magdala than in the moment when Jesus asks her two searching questions. "Woman," Jesus says, "why are you weeping? Whom are you looking for?" At a time of immense change in every aspect of our lives, including the life of the church, we need to hear our risen Lord asking these questions, especially when we find ourselves lamenting the loss of some beloved and long-treasured aspect of the faith.

Is our sense of loss—our weeping—justified? For what and for whom are we really looking? For a certain way of worship? a certain way of singing? a certain way of gathering as God's people? Are new ways of prayer, praise, and gathering really cutting us off from our Lord? Or do we feel cut off from the comfort and reassurance of familiar things?

There comes a searing moment when Mary of Magdala wishes to cling to Jesus as she knew him, only to hear and see him say that this is no longer possible. But in that same moment he offers her a relationship with his new risen reality. Her greatness as a human being allows her to rise to this deep personal challenge. It is the challenge the risen Lord poses to every Christian who is prepared to journey in faith rather than merely to remain fixed in faith.

❦ TWENTY~TWO ❦

The Encounter

Thomas (who was called the Twin), one of the twelve, was not with them when Jesus came. So the other disciples told him, "We have seen the Lord." But he said to them, "Unless I see the mark of the nails in his hands, and put my finger in the mark of the nails and my hand in his side, I will not believe." A week later his disciples were again in the house, and Thomas was with them. Although the doors were shut, Jesus came and stood among them and said, "Peace be with you." Then he said to Thomas, "Put your finger here and see my hands. Reach out your hand and put it in my side. Do not doubt but believe." Thomas answered him, "My Lord and my God!" (John 20:24–28)

You are in a strange city. You are not a city person. Your familiar world is the countryside and the lake, and both are far away to the north. You followed someone here, and that person is now dead. His death has been very public and political, and you, who know nothing about politics, suddenly find yourself involved.

Unless there is the unlikely possibility that you have family or friends here in the south, you are now on the run and have nowhere to go. To make things worse, you know that people will begin to fill the streets again as the sabbath ends, and you will become more exposed because you are a stranger from the north. Finally, as you wander aimlessly, you know that the person who means everything to you, the person who is the reason for your predicament, is lying dead in a borrowed grave less than a mile away, and you dare not go near.

There is one place that may be safe, at least for now. You recall the room in the house where you shared a meal the night before last. It is the one place known to all of you, the one place where you are most likely to find the others. Yet something prevents you from going there.

You suddenly realize that you don't want the company of others at this time. You have come to see them all in their utter humanity. The ox-like dullness of Peter, the crass self-interest of James and John, the sheep-like passivity of others, their inability to grasp anything of the vision Jesus offered, and above all the utter treachery of Judas. Everything about them reminds you of the cause and relationship to which you gave yourself and which transformed your life, giving it purpose and meaning. You had such great hope for it all. In giving yourself you had found yourself, and now all that is utterly destroyed. You want no echoes of a voice, no reminders of past days.

You suddenly realize that you are near the house where you are almost certain they have gathered to wait out the rest of this awful Sabbath day. You have only to walk the last steps, go up the outer stairs, knock at the door, and say quietly to the listener inside, "It's Thomas." But instead, you turn and risk yourself to the city streets.

One day your friend John will remember that you were not with the disciples that sabbath day. When you do decide to join them a few days later, and they try to persuade you of what has happened in your absence, you will feel only contempt for their credulity and self-persuasion. But something makes you stay with them against your better judgment, and there comes a moment when you encounter what you thought you had lost. You stretch out your hand to touch, and your broken heart is healed.

Most people who read John's gospel assume that Thomas had indeed joined the disciples but happened to be away for a short while when Jesus came among them. I have suggested that he had chosen not to join them because he had to be alone to deal with the depth of his loss.

Far from being a doubter—the description forever attached to his name—Thomas is the consummate disciple, the one who gives himself utterly. Those of us who have given ourselves deeply and generously to a cause can often withdraw from participation when something happens to change, and therefore—in our view—to diminish, the object of our loyalty.

We decide that we no longer wish the associations and relationships that issued from that loyalty. So much has been at stake, so much of ourselves has been invested, so deeply has it penetrated the fabric of our lives, that we cannot bear to be reminded of what once gave meaning to much of our time and energy. We can even find ourselves blaming the community itself for the things with which it struggles.

In church life a common phenomenon is the church-warden who ends years of office and is never seen again in church. She or he may have been through very difficult times and issues, and may have performed with magnificent competence, but something has happened to break the bond with congregational life. It may be that there is a continued personal faithfulness to our Lord, but an aversion to the life of the worshipping community.

Sometimes this may result simply from burnout. We are tired of trying to resolve endless struggles between differing opinions and factions. But sometimes the cause is deeper. Perhaps we have a sense of disappointment with the church, a feeling not so much that we must leave it as that somehow it has left us. Perhaps we expected less unpleasantness than we had found in other worlds we move in, among them our professional world. Perhaps we expected people to behave differently, be more forgiving, more able to live together. Little by little we came to see the church as the problem, or at least a large part of the problem. And so there came a day when we discovered that life was perfectly livable without something we once treasured and even loved.

Time would show that Thomas desperately wanted to believe in Jesus. When given the chance, he blurted out his steadfast faithfulness. In today's society there are innumerable men and women lost to the worshipping community who have not lost a personal faith. It is sad that this link is often severed precisely at a stage of life when we need a community where we can find friendship that is freely offered, support when we need it, and a purpose in living.

There would come a moment in the next few days when Thomas would walk down the street, climb the steps, knock on the door, wait for the voice inside to ask his name, and respond, "It's Thomas." Very soon after that he would kneel before the One who needs no door to enter, and say, "My Lord and my God."

For Thomas, a return to the community was the way to an encounter with the Risen Christ. May it be so for us.

TWENTY THREE

Flight and Return

*Now on that same day two of them were going to a village
called Emmaus, about seven miles from Jerusalem, and talking with each other about all these things that had happened.
While they were talking and discussing, Jesus himself came
near and went with them, but their eyes were kept from
recognizing him.... As they came near the village to which
they were going, he walked ahead as if he were going on. But
they urged him strongly, saying, "Stay with us, because it is
almost evening and the day is now nearly over." So he went
in to stay with them. When he was at the table with them,
he took bread, blessed and broke it, and gave it to them.
Then their eyes were opened, and they recognized him; and
he vanished from their sight.... That same hour they got up
and returned to Jerusalem; and they found the eleven and
their companions gathered together. They were saying, "The
Lord has risen indeed, and he has appeared to Simon!" Then
they told what had happened on the road, and how he had
been made known to them in the breaking of the bread.*
(Luke 24:13–16, 28–31, 33–35)

In the long hours of this devastating weekend, there would have been some argument among the disciples about the wisest course of action. Many in the community were far from home and would need to consider their livelihood—working lives can be interrupted for only so long.

There would have been discussions about safety. They were not only outsiders in a highly political city, but were now associated with a movement deemed subversive and dangerous by determined authorities. Some would have advised a quick escape north to Galilee and the familiar world of the lake. Others would have counselled staying in the area, if only for a short while, to remain near the place where Jesus had died.

We know what Cleopas and another did. They decided to leave the city behind and head for the village of Emmaus. Luke does not say why they choose Emmaus. Perhaps it was home for one of them, or at least a place where they could be assured of welcome and shelter.

On their journey they discuss their agonizing loss, and they encounter a stranger who enquires about their conversation. Immediately Cleopas releases all the pent-up sorrow and anger he is feeling. How can this stranger not know their loss? How can he not be aware of all they had so desperately hoped for, worked for, risked for? Calmly and deliberately the stranger responds. They hear their own history laid out for them in a way that makes perfect sense of what they have experienced.

They are suddenly aware of having almost reached their destination. They don't want to lose the company of this companion who inspires so much quiet confidence. As they sit at one of the inn's tables to eat with their guest, he takes a piece of bread and breaks it. Suddenly, inexplicably, they know him. They are speechless, shocked, confused. It is one of those moments almost impossible to recapture when it has past, impossible to exactly recall the events or the order of events. When they look for him, he has gone.

The next few hours see them on the road to Jerusalem. Threading their way through the narrow alleys of the city, they reach the house where they know some of the community is still hiding. Before they can utter a word, ecstatic voices around them announce, "The Lord has risen indeed, and he has appeared to Simon!" Their own breathless account of their experience in the inn on the edge of Emmaus brings more excited responses. At this moment, through the babble of voices, a calm familiar voice is heard saying, "Peace be with you."

In this scripture we walk with these two disciples as they journey to Emmaus and return to Jerusalem. With them we pass from sorrow and loss to joy and celebration. It is a journey that most of us take in one form or another as we move through the infinitely varied experiences of our lives.

We may not yet have suffered such devastating loss in our lives, but we have probably known lesser losses, and we have had to distance ourselves for a while to recover, before returning to engage life. We may have lost a position of employment. We may have left a relationship that had become impossible. We may have walked away from the earthly remains of someone we loved above everything and everyone else in this world.

In all these differing journeys we will have walked with many conflicting feelings—great bitterness, deep regret, almost inexpressible grief. Like the two on the Emmaus road, if we were asked why we felt this way, we may have reacted with anger. How can anyone not know our loss or sorrow? Surely others must feel it!

Yet even as we read these words, we know that it is possible to return from whatever sad journeys we may have taken. Many have been given grace and strength to pick up the pieces. Some who have walked away from faith have come again to renewed faith. Others who have known the pain of a failed relationship have found again the joy of friendship or love. Even those who have tasted the greatest losses in life have been enabled to turn again to living.

Grace to make possible such return journeys can come from many sources, but whatever the immediate source may be, the deepest source is the mystery we call resurrection. This mystery dwells at the heart of Christian faith, and finds embodiment in Jesus.

When the two companions returned to that long-ago Jerusalem, they searched instinctively for the community that had grown through loyalty and affection for Jesus. The two who burst in on the group were at pains to say how exactly they had recognized the risen Jesus. It was, they said, in the moment when he had broken bread at the inn table.

Many who have experienced great loss or sorrow have found new life in the setting of a Christian community. Here they have heard the name of the risen Christ spoken, felt the bread of his body placed in their outstretched hands and, restored and strengthened, have returned to fullness of life.

TWENTY-FOUR

Epilogue

What then are we to say about these things? If God is for us, who is against us? He who did not withhold his own Son, but gave him up for all of us, will he not with him also give us everything else? ... For I am convinced that neither death, nor life, nor angels, nor rulers, nor things present, nor things to come, nor powers, nor height, nor depth, nor anything else in all creation, will be able to separate us from the love of God in Christ Jesus our Lord. (Romans 8:31-32, 38-39)

We have shared four crucial days in the lives of those men and women who experienced the birth of what would come to be called Christian faith. Many of us who read these pages now share that faith and hold it in our lives as something precious and grace giving.

The disciples would have other encounters with the risen Jesus in the weeks following these four days in spring. Eventually they would realize the inevitability of his presence being withdrawn from them, to be replaced by the knowledge that he was alive in each of them as an individual, and in the network of relationships, beliefs, commitments, and tasks that would one day be called the church.

Some years after these four days, when communities across the eastern Mediterranean were beginning slowly and with much struggle to recognize themselves as a single body of faithful people, Paul the apostle, writing to one such community in the city of Corinth, reminded them of the many appearances of the risen Lord of which he himself was aware.

I handed on to you as of first importance what I in turn had received: that Christ died for our sins in accordance with the scriptures, and that he was buried, and that he was raised on the third day in accordance with the scriptures, and that he appeared to Cephas, then to the twelve. Then he appeared to more than five hundred brothers and sisters at one time, most of whom are still alive, though some have died. Then he appeared to James, then to all the apostles. Last of all, as to one untimely born, he appeared also to me.

Among the extraordinary phenomena of history is the way that an insignificant minority of men and women exploded on to the stage of the Roman Empire in the early days of its imperial power. Within a century they had grown into a minority significant enough to affect its life. Within two centuries they had become a political force, and within three centuries they had inherited the now weakening empire.

If we could ask them what had made that extraordinary achievement possible, they would give us an answer that has become almost incomprehensible to many people twenty-one centuries later. They would say, "The resurrection of our Lord Jesus Christ!" Many today, if they were to hear this reply, would assume that perhaps those early Christians had not heard our question. How can a religious belief—which in our Western culture has become private and personal—initiate a social and political movement that is capable of taking over an empire?

There is considerable irony in this last statement. We are the first generation in the Western world for centuries who are living with a religious belief that has nurtured a vast civilization, and that affects us in an extremely troubling way. This new reality is the world of Islam that sprang from the personal vision of the prophet Muhammad. How is it possible that the crucifixion and resurrection of Jesus Christ became such an engine of political and social change, yet has become in our time a private religious belief, held only by those who choose to believe it, and with little significance outside the private spiritual domain?

First of all, even those who were changed forever by the Christian faith could not explain it. If we could question them, we would be frustrated. They would say to us again and again, "He is alive! We don't know how! All we know is that he is alive. And so, in a way we simply don't understand, we are more alive!" Responses like this frustrated the intellectuals of that long-ago time. Repeatedly we hear fine Greek and Roman minds expressing frustration and even contempt for this new faith. For many of them it was inexplicable and unreasonable—at best a delusion, at worst a conspiracy. All these opinions sound very contemporary. All are at least twenty centuries old.

The extraordinary new energy of the Christian faith continued to reshape the classical world until, for better and for worse, the Eastern empire that would one day be called Byzantium hitched its future to Christian faith, and the rest is history—a checkered history that cannot claim to be perfect, but that has proven to be breathtakingly energetic and creative.

When the Western empire collapsed in the fifth century, the idea of a risen Christ flowered in the islands of the Atlantic. It inspired some of the greatest illuminated manuscripts the world has seen. It galvanized Celtic monks into preserving the same classical culture the empire was rapidly losing. It triggered the founding of monastic communities from Iceland to Kiev. And those communities formed outposts of civilization in a Western Europe that had become the domain of warlords and savagery.

In the High Middle Ages this same theme of resurrection raised the loveliness of Chartres and Cologne and York cathedrals. They became powerhouses of artistic and intellectual energy. Later still in the movement we call the Renaissance, some of the world's most enduring art formed around the themes of the passion and resurrection of Jesus Christ.

The record is not perfect. We are dealing with humanity. Christian faith takes tragic detours. The Crusades do their slaughtering. The Inquisition brings approaches to interrogation still perpetrated today. There are chapters of virulent anti-Semitism. There are, as always, Christian voices who speak in terms of conquest. In the seventeenth century there will be such vicious religious wars that subsequent generations will turn to rationality and the sciences as a saner way to build a society.

By the eighteenth century the Enlightenment will have begun to relegate Christian faith to the domain of the personal and the private. By the late twentieth century Christian faith will be largely excluded from what has come to be called "the public square," and will have become something valid only in the church, the home, and the privacy of individual experience. But, in spite of all these things,

> From the Assisi countryside, Francis will speak to Europe of a way of gentleness and compassion.
>
> Dante will write the great journey through Heaven, Hell, and Purgatory—*The Divine Comedy*.
>
> George Herbert's poetry will shine out of an England embroiled in religious struggle.
>
> From Johann Sebastian Bach will pour forth more than three hundred sacred cantatas.
>
> Elizabeth Fry will wed her quiet Quaker spirituality to a will of steel and begin the reforming of the British prison system.
>
> Teresa and her sisters will pick up bodies from the streets of Calcutta.
>
> Jean Vanier will open the doors of L'Arche to the handicapped.
>
> Desmond Tutu will form the Truth and Reconciliation Commission of South Africa.
>
> John Tavener will write his incomparable music linking Western and Orthodox spirituality.

Every one of these people—and many more beyond numbering—if they were asked for the source of moral and artistic energy in their lives, would speak of the resurrected Christ.

One particular image may give us an impression of the countless ways that the resurrection of our Lord Jesus Christ has formed, focused, and energized human thought and action. A great painting of the Renaissance, "Resurrection" by Piero della Francesca, is an almost universally known icon. In this magnificent canvas we see how the resurrection of Christ has begun to take on what we today would call ecological significance. The figure of Christ, occupying the centre of the picture, rises majestically from the tomb. All other human figures lie stunned or asleep. In the background is a stretch of countryside. To the left, all nature is dead, locked in a barren winter. To the right of Christ's head, all trees and vegetation are alive and blossoming in a passionate spring.

A voice from the twenty-first century echoes in words what della Francesca shows us on canvas. Sister Elizabeth Johnson of Fordham University writes,

> A flourishing humanity on a thriving Earth in an evolving universe, all together filled with the glory of God; such is the theological vision and praxis we are being called to in this critical age of Earth's distress.... This moment of crisis calls for a spirituality and ethics that will empower us to live in the web of life as sustainers rather than destroyers of the world.... Instead of living as thoughtless or greedy exploiters of the earth, we, by conversion to the Earth, are empowered to rediscover our kinship and live as sisters and brothers, friends and lovers, mothers and fathers, priests and prophets, co-creators and children of the Earth as God's good creation gives us life.

Here the power of the resurrection displays itself as more than personal religion, valid and important though this may be. Here we are speaking of nothing less than the resurrection of the natural order—our environment.

In writing these pages I have tried to witness to the power of our Lord's passion and resurrection. I have attempted to show that, when we hear or say the words "Christ is risen," we are making a statement that encompasses every facet of human experience—personal, social, political, ecological. My prayer is that of Saint Paul, written in his letter to the Christian community in Ephesus. He writes, "I pray that you may have the power to comprehend, with all the saints, what is the breadth and length and height and depth, and to know the love of Christ that surpasses knowledge."

Victoria, B.C.
2006

Path Books
A LIGHT TO MY PATH

We hope that you have enjoyed reading this Path Book. For more information about Path Books, please visit our web site at www.pathbooks.com. If you have comments or suggestions about Path Books, please write us at publisher@pathbooks.com.

Other Path Books

Finer than Gold, Sweeter than Honey: The Psalms for Our Living
by Herbert O'Driscoll
The psalms are among the most sublime poetry in the world, offering us inexhaustible wells of meaning. Herbert O'Driscoll dips into their sacred depths and draws up sparkling insights to refresh the soul. The reader will find rewarding suggestions for personal reflection, daily journalling, group discussion, and sermon preparation.
1-55126-449-8 soft cover, 309 pp., $26.95

God With Us: The Companionship of Jesus in the Challenges of Life
by Herbert O'Driscoll
In 33 perceptive meditations, Herbert O'Driscoll considers the challenges of being human, searches key events in the life of Jesus, and discovers new vitality and guidance for our living, showing us how the healing wisdom and power of Jesus' life can transform our own lives today.
1-55126-359-9 soft cover, 173 pp., $18.95

Living Scripture: The Guidance of God on the Journey of Life by Herbert O'Driscoll
Where can we find truly inspiring models of leadership, friendship, creativity, and humanity to guide and motivate us? Reflecting on 29 well-known biblical characters — including Moses, Bathsheba, Naomi, Pilate, and Jesus himself — O'Driscoll shows how their strivings to live wisely, fully, and joyfully have relevance for our lives today.
1-55126-436-6 soft cover, 158 pp., $18.95